PRODUCT OF COLOMBIA

A son's Story

Dago Ivan Rodriguez

Dăgo: he who supplants (victory)

SILVERSMITH
PRESS

Published by Silversmith Press–Houston, Texas
www.silversmithpress.com

978-1-961093-90-4 (Softcover Book)
978-1-961093-91-1 (eBook)
978-1-967386-47-5 (Spanish)

Yea, though I walk through the valley of the shadow of death, I will fear no evil: for thou art with me; thy rod and thy staff they comfort me.

PSALMS 23:4

Contents

PROLOGUE

The News

For the thing which I greatly feared is come upon me,
And that which I was afraid of is come unto me.

JOB 3:25

Florida 1998

In a single moment, my worst fears had come to pass.
Never had I felt such pain and loss piercing through
every cell of my body. I heard the most agonizing
scream erupt from within. I had just expelled every
ounce of pain I had in me.

All the stereotyping, all the judgment and sneers
caused by our family secret had just come to fru-
ition. It had reached its logical conclusion. But,
strangely enough, though it seemed I had fallen
into a vast internal void, I could feel my heart-
beat once again as if for the first time. It was
hard to imagine that, through this piercing dou-
ble-edged sword, I would come to a place of solace
and redemption.

Eight years after that dreadful day, I find myself on a bus on my way to meet my baby sister, now twelve years old. Feeling anxious but excited, I can only imagine what she may be thinking and how our first meeting will go … but I'm getting ahead of myself.

Let me take you back to how my complex journey all started and how I am a product of my upbringing with the intervention of grace.

Raised Tough

Hear, O LORD, when I cry with my voice:
Have mercy also upon me and answer me.

PSALM 27:7

Colombia, South America, 1968

I can recall myself as a three-year-old sitting at my grandmother's front doorstep staring at all the kids in the park. With them were adult male figures that I did not understand at the time were their fathers.

I would always wonder what it would be like to have someone like that in m life. Growing up, I felt cheated at not having what seemed so special and comforting to all the other kids in that park. So I rebelled and acted out in the best way I could by using the only thing I knew to use—words. I would use them to hurt all of my loved ones, lashing out at my aunts and uncles, but mostly my precious maternal grandmother Abigail. She never deserved any of my abuse but somehow would always keep her patience with me. At the time, I didn't understand why she had so much patience with me, but I am grateful for the gentle love that she always showed me.

I can only imagine how my father Dágoberto might have turned out if he'd had the same love and understanding growing up. It was a stark contrast. When his mother admitted to her husband that Dágo was not his son, she was forced to throw my father out of the house at the tender age of seven. He was out in the streets having to fend for himself. What thoughts must have been going through the mind of this defenseless young boy, unloved, homeless, lost, and abandoned by the very woman that had brought him into the world!

At such a young age he was forced to grow up very quickly, and on the streets of Roncesvalles, Colombia, he figured out a way to survive. He would teach himself how to read and write and, although the odds were not in his favor, he developed into a quiet, brave young man with the most graceful penmanship one had ever seen. More importantly, he would teach himself how to sing and play the guitar, and from there, music would become his outlet and a way to deal with his pain.

Singing and playing his guitar, he could hold any-one captive, mesmerized by the sheer beauty and pathos in his voice. I always remember as a little boy leaving all the other kids behind to go watch him sing and play his guitar at every family gathering. I was always front row and center, hypnotized by such pain and emotion coming out of this man that I called my father. At the time I didn't understand how for him, a modest man of few words, this was his way of dealing with emotions hidden deep down inside and the only way he dared to share his pain with anyone.

I believe this was the reason why so many who watched him perform connected so deeply with him because he sang with the same pain we all have hidden somewhere deep inside.

It was this talent and pain coupled with his good looks and silent noble charisma that won my mother's heart after his persistent serenading of her with the song "La malagueña" at the front door of my grandmother's house. I still have the very guitar that won my mother's heart; it's one of the most cherished keepsake I hold of my parents love for one another. He would also go on to steal grand-mother Abigail's heart and she would grow very fond of him and become a sort of mother figure to him, treating him like one of her own. He would reciprocate and treat her with the same honor and respect you would a loving mother. They became inseparable and would always go out of their way for one another.

On one occasion my father overheard that the mayor's son had also become very fond of my mother. There were rumors that he was going to propose as well. Well, this did not sit right with my father and he decided to seek him out and have a talk with him. But with emotions flying and their honor at stake, it did not take much for things to turn out badly for both of them. The mayor's son ended up with a bruised ego as well as quite a few extra bumps and bruises after being knocked out by my father's infamous left cross. The town had actually placed a fine on his left arm every time he would knock someone out with it. On the outside, he was this humble, quiet, unassuming man but he was known to never back down from a fight and, at that age, there were plenty of chances to prove his bravado. This time was no exception and my father would end up paying for that left cross in the local jail for a week.

Well, when my grandmother Abigail found out what happened, she made sure to go see him every day and bring him food and cigarettes. Not your conventional bonding for either of them, but their strong fondness and love for one another would endure beyond what anybody could expect.

La Violencia

Colombia's Civil War

"La Violencia" was a ten year civil war from 1948 to 1958 in Colombia, which polarized the entire country. Soon my father would find himself fighting for his beliefs and his country. He was a very courageous and proficient soldier and was even given the nickname "Relámpago" which is Spanish for "lightning" because he was such a fast and accurate marksmen.

On one occasion, he was trekking through the jungle with another soldier, and they decided to take a break. They sat down to rest on a log but the log rolled them off and moved away. To their amazement, they realized they had been sitting on what was actually an enormous anaconda. After a good laugh and much relief, they were thankful they hadn't become the snake's next meal. I recall this story with fondness simply because it was shared with me by my father himself on one of the rare occasions he actually shared anything about himself with me.

Soon enough though, efforts to call an end to all the violence between both political parties would be successful and many, including my father, would return to their former lives.

My father had always been a very gifted animal lover and as the war was coming to an end he became the local veterinarian. He was very passionate and capable in his newfound profession. He eventually became certified and was able to maintain a modest living for himself and my mother after they were married and had their first child, a little girl named Astrid Leonora.

Tragically, my sister would only live for a few weeks. At the hands of my father's mother, she would develop pneumonia after being bathed outside in the cold mountain air, and would not survive. My mother was devastated. She was having a difficult time coping with the loss of her first child, so my grandmother Abigail advised my father that having another child as soon as possible would help ease my mother's sense of loss. My father took her advice. Once my mother started to feel her new child growing, it brought her back into a new state of hope and joy. That second child was me and, from what I've been told and seen in pictures, I was showered with love and affection by both of my parents. Fortunately, I would remember those precious moments at my mother's funeral—a very poignant time in my life.

Soon after, my father moved us to the capitol of Colombia, Bogota, in pursuit of a better life. In the past he had worked as a bodyguard for one of the local emerald cartel figures of the time. But, he would return to one of his former jobs as a taxi driver, which had always provided for us and now would allow him to make the move to Bogota and save up for his chance at new opportunities far away from the tentacles of his family. This was something that he had always struggled with because, although he loved his family and yearned for their love and respect, he would always end up on the losing end of things with his family. This was always hard for him to deal with especially coming from his own mother.

My father had struggled and fought hard to become the man he had now become—his own person without a family by his side when he most needed them. He had survived a civil war and the devastating loss of a child at the hands of his own mother. But now, he was close to making a clean break in North America, the "U S of A, land of opportunity," or so he thought.

America!

A Strange New Place

As I look back, I can only imagine what it must have been like to leave everything he knew behind: family, a language you understand and the people you love and identify with. And yet he let it all go to get to a place that was not his own to be looked upon as a total stranger, not belonging in the eyes of these new people. I have personally found it hard just to move across town, let alone to a new country where you can't even speak the language or understand the customs.

What would make someone leave everything and everyone he knew for so much risk and change? I can only wonder what all the past immigrants had to endure leaving their own countries and stepping into the unknown with new visions of possibilities they could only dream of. I was not fortunate enough to experience this for myself but I am grateful to my father for his courage and for taking that leap of faith for me.

My father arrived in New York in the late 60s with a determination to start a new life far away from all the snares and temptations of his past. On arrival, he was fortunate enough to stay with cousins on my mother's side, Fabio and Margarita, until he got on his feet. It was a different time, but they guided him towards getting his permanent residency and sending for my mother.

Soon after arriving, he was able to find work at a car dealership as an assistant in the paint and body department. There he developed a friendship with a fellow Colombian by the name of Octavio who taught him the auto body and paint trade. This was something he became very skilled at as well as passionate about. And his new friendship with Octavio would develop into a great and lasting one. Things were starting to come together for him in America and soon he was able to send for my mother. Once my mother arrived, she found a job in a factory and was able to help save for a bigger place for the arrival of my newly born brother—and to send for me.

Meanwhile, I was still in Colombia making my aunts and uncles miserable by testing their patience every single day. No one got it worse than my grandmother Abigail, who continued to be the most patient with me. I used to love going to the local marketplace with her every morning to buy the daily provisions for her to make our breakfast, lunch and dinner. She would do this in between her daily appointments in her home-based dental practice. She was a remarkable woman, but I couldn't understand where she got such drive and energy to provide for all five of us that lived with her and two uncles that would religiously stop by on their lunch breaks to visit. I learned so much from her especially on our early morning walks to the market. She would constantly make me smile and feel loved as she shared her life lessons and wisdom in her own Abigail way. But, most importantly, she would always leave me thinking about the stories she shared with me from the Bible.

In the short time I was with my grandmother, I learned many lessons that I am deeply grateful for. The most important one was to always have dignity for myself and others. I truly miss those walks with her and cherish every moment we shared.

Soon my father sent for me and my dear grand-mother helped pack my things and sent me off to the airport. I would fly to America for the first time accompanied by my father's brother. This is the first time I would be away from my grandmother and my uncles and aunts. Uncle Alfonso and Aunt Marta, who were like older brothers, and aunts Deicy and Amparo who had been like mothers to me since my mother left for America. And, had I known that twenty years later my aunt Deicy would once again be my rock in this new country, I would have treated her more kindly than I did. To be honest, I wish I had treated all my aunts and uncles with a lot more respect and love before I left.

On the flight over I wasn't really feeling anything, to be honest, I didn't know what to feel or to expect, I guess I was sort of numb and maybe still a little angry at my dad for "abandoning" me.

Once we landed in New York, my father was there to pick us up and, as we approached the baggage area, my uncle turned to me and said, "This is your father." As I looked up at him, I mustered up all my bottled-up resentment and anger and looked up at this man that I didn't recognize or feel anything for him but anger, and said the most hurtful words I could put together. From the look on his face and the watering of his eyes, I could tell that my words had accomplished what I intended them to do. I was angry and hurt and I wanted him to know it. Why wasn't he around when I most needed him to take me to the park and walk with me and show me off proudly like all the other fathers at that park with their boys?

Unconsciously, I must have been preparing for that moment. When it arrived and I saw the hurt I had caused in him, I realized how much more it had hurt me than made me feel better. I truly didn't want to hurt my father and now, looking back, I realize he didn't deserve what I had said to him; but at the time I just wished he had been there when I most needed him. Now I realize I could not expect him to know that when he never had a father of his own to teach him how to be a father to me. All he was doing was making a sacrifice to provide a better life for us, and it wouldn't be until much later in life that I would realize how much he truly sacrificed for our family.

During the ride home from the airport, not a word was said that I can remember. When I entered my new home and saw my mother—for what I thought at the time was my first time because I had no memory of either of my parents—I was so excited. I went from feeling abandoned to feeling overjoyed because I finally had parents and a place I could call home. I instantly had a family and I felt like I finally belonged. And, if that was not enough, my mother told me to go into the bedroom and see the present that was there

waiting for me. As I walked in, I saw the most ador-
able little baby boy just a few months old and then
my mother tells me that he was my brother Eddie.
At that moment I felt totally complete and still do to
this day. That was truly the happiest day of my life.

Well, that euphoria did not last very long. Being
the rebellious little boy that got away with anything
I wanted back in Colombia, I immediately went back
to my hyperactive and uncontrollable self. I started
to jump on the furniture and yell and scream. Thank
God for the lesson I was about to learn that night.
My father was not having all the screaming and was
not going to put up with my outbursts, so he gently
told me to stop yelling and jumping on the furniture.
But, because nobody had ever stopped me before, I
thought I could keep doing and acting like I always
had. But not in my father's house! I quickly learned
that there were rules and consequences here. After
the third time telling me to behave and stop jumping
on the furniture and being ignored, he quickly taught
me about respect.

I looked up at my father with wide eyes as he took
off his belt and folded it twice and laid me over his
lap. Then gently, but with enough sting, he landed a
couple of whacks on my bottom. Boy, did that get my

attention! I was terrified watching him take off his belt because no one had ever disciplined me before. I know now that subconsciously even at that age I understood why he was doing this.

I don't believe that I cried—not that I can remember—but I do remember being quiet and shocked. Somehow though, I felt loved. I believe it was because someone had finally taken the time to teach me how to be a respectful little boy. It must have been the reason for my acting out all those times. It is as if I understood subconsciously that there is a correlation between discipline and love, and that day I learned a most valuable lesson that changed me for the better.

Soon after, my grandmother Abigail suffered a heart attack and I was sent back briefly to be with her as she was asking to see me once again. When I arrived, all my aunts and uncles were puzzled, and wondering who this little boy was. They could not believe how loving and well-behaved I was. No more filthy hurtful words being hurled at them; instead a polite boy who would actually listen to them. And my out-of-control hyperactive episodes were a thing of the past. This allowed for better relationships between us all and I was much happier for it. I had been given the opportunity to show my family how much they meant to me, how much I loved them, especially my dear grandmother Abigail who, God bless her, never ever deserved my outbursts and disrespect.

My stay back in Colombia was brief. As soon as my grandmother recuperated, I flew back to my mother and father in New York. Soon after, we moved to New Jersey where I started school. My first experience with school was not pleasant at all. I remember feeling lost, not knowing where I was supposed to go and how to ask for directions because I did not speak the language yet. My parents were no better at speaking English, so I pretty much had to learn to fend for myself the best I could.

It took a few times to find my way to where I was supposed to be but, once in the right classroom, I felt like I was invisible. Nobody cared, not even the teachers. I remember one day I just walked out of class and no one stopped me as I went out to the playground and climbed up on the monkey bars. Once I had climbed up to the top, I pretended to be a sky diver and jumped off and in mid-flight I reached to pull my parachute's rip cord. As I did, I hit the ground and broke my left arm in two places. So being the independent boy I was learning to be, I didn't go back into the school to ask for help—well, I was too embarrassed and scared anyway, plus I couldn't speak the language. So, I gently picked my left arm up and held it up against my chest all the way back home where I waited all day on the steps of the front door for my mother and father to come home from work.

I never learned much at that school except how to stand up for myself. One morning as I was walking to school passing by the local cemetery, three bigger boys, maybe from middle or even high school, jumped me, hung me upside down and shook all my lunch money out of my pockets. I remember being so angry especially at lunch time when I realized how hungry I was. The next morning again on my way to school at the exact same spot, the same three kids jumped out, held me up and took my money once again. This time, I was so angry and hungry at lunch time that I made up my mind that no matter what, they weren't taking my money ever again. By the third day, I had built up so much anger and frustration that I was hoping they would try it again. Sure enough, there they were and tried once again to take my money; but this time I was over it and too angry and fed up to let them take it. With my little Latin blood boiling, I somehow fended them off. This time they realized it wasn't going to be so easy, and they let me go. It felt good to have stood my ground and be able to keep my lunch money. I was so happy when lunch time came around and I was able to sit down and eat. I could recall the scuffle with a gleam in my eye.

The next morning and every morning thereafter as I walked by the same spot, they no longer jumped out but instead stayed hidden behind the same bushes and would just wave as I walked on by waiting for some other easy prey. That's the day I learned the value of standing up for myself, and it would serve me well the rest of my life.

Hot and Humid Florida

One summer break my father took us on a vacation down to Disney World, Florida. I hated it. I couldn't believe how hot and humid Florida was. It wasn't fun either sweating out there waiting in line to get on rides. While we were there, my father was tricked into a free trip and show in southwest Florida's Waltzing Waters dolphin show if he listened to one of their sales pitches. He came out of that meeting buying property with access to the river. This was important to him because he loved being around water, boating and fishing.

So, once back in New Jersey, they started making plans to move to Florida permanently. I wasn't so excited about moving. But, soon after arriving in Jersey, my mother had fallen down a flight of stairs and injured her back. Being in traction for what seemed a long stay in the hospital put my father in a financial bind. He found himself having to reach out to his side of the family, mainly his mother and sister for help. They did, and soon my mother was able to get out of the hospital, although still not walking or feeling very well. Her condition kept worsening and so my father was forced to send her back to Colombia to see if any doctors there could operate on her injured lower back. A well known doctor who came highly recommended was finally able to see her. He recommended surgery to relieve the pain that the ruptured disc was causing and inhibiting her from walking normal again.

Before the surgery, my mother and the rest of the family were extremely worried because it was a very new and delicate procedure, and there was no guarantee she would ever walk again. Yet, by the grace of God, the surgery was a success and the doctor was very pleased with her recovery. Soon she would be finishing her rehab and coming home to my grandmother and eventually back home to America. This for me, would be a glimpse of my mother's strength and courage in taking on what she was confronted with in life.

Once back home in New Jersey, my aunt Deicy flew in to help take care of her as well as my brother and me, since my mother was still struggling to regain her mobility. It took a while, but she was so determined to walk on her own without the help of a cane or walker so much that she never stopped pushing herself to walk without any assistance. She was truly a courageous and strong woman; but at the time, I did not comprehend just how much.

As my mother started to recuperate and walk again, they continued with plans to move to Florida and we would eventually find ourselves driving down south. I wasn't sure what to expect, but the closer we got into the southwest of Florida, the more it started to reaffirm my aversion to living there. It was just as hot and humid as I remembered and full of mosquitoes that seemed to be having a drunken feast at my expense. I was also not a fan of the palmetto bugs (a nice way to describe flying cockroaches) that seemed to make their home in almost every palm tree. And another native to keep an eye out for was the local alligators. I was not a big fan of them as well but I learned what a delicacy they could be once I got older.

Like it or not, we all settled into our new home and my brother and I started to enjoy more of the out-doors, although still hating the humidity. One day we made such a racket outside that our next door neighbors a retired couple would call the police on us for playing too loudly with our toy trucks. At first I couldn't understand what was going on, why the police were there talking to us, especially since we couldn't understand a word they were saying. But I think they finally figured it out and left.

It was kinda shocking but this wasn't out of the ordinary for this little southern town of Cape Coral that was designated specifically for retirees. I remember a local ordinance that the city was trying to pass that would make it mandatory for every-one living within the city limits to have white-wall tires on their cars. Thinking back, I still can't believe that this retirement community was trying to pass such a nonsensical ordinance even if it was in the early 1970s.

Nonetheless, this was the place we had come to call home. It was populated mostly by retirees, which in a way, was a blessing in disguise because it was a quiet and peaceful place to grow up in. We also met some very special neighbors that became like family who always looked out for us, and my parents would make sure to return the favor and keep a close eye on them as well.

One neighbor, in particular, a retiree from Canada, would become like a dear grandmother to us. We came to love our dear neighbor Kathy very much because of her generous heart and the love she always showed our whole family. She was never judgmental and never stereotyped us because of who we were; she just accepted us as good people and neighbors.

My first time trying to get on a bus to school proved to be more difficult than I imagined. As it turned out, I actually got on the wrong bus and ended going clear over to the next town ending up in a middle school of all places. Who would have thought that a little boy would actually be allowed onto the wrong bus and in the wrong school without any adults stepping in! It's funny now but it sure didn't seem funny at the time. Eventually someone noticed that I was a bit too young and decided to help me. They finally figured it out without either one of us speaking the other's language. Thank goodness people here in Florida still cared and went out of their way to sort it all out. It was a stark difference from the apathetic attitude I had experienced back in New Jersey. When I finally made it to the elementary school, thanks to a caring adult that drove me back across town, I felt a whole lot less out of place.

Learning English!

I quickly settled in and, over the next few months, I finally started to feel like I mattered and somebody cared. I had spent two years in first grade back in New Jersey and still didn't understand a word of English. The only two words I could say were yes and no and I usually got them mixed up, ha that was always fun. At this new school they explained to my parents that I was too old to be held back for a second time and so they placed me in second grade in a remedial class, which I am so grateful for. Within just a few months I could speak, read, and write in English for the first time, and it felt great. Along with this new grasp of the English language, I quickly became the family translator anytime my parents needed help communicating in English.

I was really enjoying reading and so my father bought us a set of encyclopedias from a traveling sales lady Mariela, who would later became a dear friend of the family. I read everything that I could in that set of encyclopedias. I could not put them down. I wanted to learn everything I could especially now that we had our own. I was particularly interested in airplanes, motorcycle, automobiles and electronics. And, when I wasn't reading or daydreaming about them, I was driving my dad's friend Octavio crazy every chance I could asking him all about how engines worked.

Octavio had also moved his family to south Florida, and my father and he became inseparable. We were like one big family and their two sons John and Steve would become so close that to this day we think of ourselves as cousins. We learned to hunt birds, fish and ride minibikes as well as getting into occasional fist fights with each other. Those were some great memories and all part of growing up boys learning how to be tough and stand our ground. Having friends close to our own age was important, especially ones that spoke the same language.

My Bike and Me

My parents soon enrolled me in "Futball" or as Americans call it "Soccer." You would have thought that being from Colombia, I would have been a natural at it, but on the contrary, I was awful and did not enjoy it, especially all the running around chasing a ball. My parents quickly realized my disdain for my country's national sport and decided to enroll me in basketball. But just as you imagined, I was not any better at it but I did enjoy it. I played for a season but then grew out of it and moved on to taekwondo, where I was much happier at learning how to defend myself. I also enjoyed my time as a Webelos Scout but soon I would find my true passion—two wheels. I could not get enough of riding my bicycle. I would ride all day long during my summer breaks. Growing up with Evel Knievel as my hero, I tried breaking all his records, in my mind and on my bicycle along with a few broken bones and many broken bicycles—not mine—that my father had to constantly repair.

Finally, my dad and I decided that I would design and he would weld me up a bicycle frame using parts from some of our spare mini bikes. I also persuaded him to weld up a go-kart frame that I had designed. He never said no and always took the time to go along with my motorsport schemes. That same day, he surprised my brother and me with a quick rip down the street next to the body shop he was working at on a Saturday morning. The shop was closed and it was just the three of us. We were accompanying our dad while he caught up on some work. Next thing we know we found ourselves strapped into the safety harnesses of a beautiful blue, white striped 1968 Shelby GT500 Mustang with our dad at the controls of this beast of a car while we fishtailed side to side pouring smoke out of the rear fenders and laid an endless tire mark all the way down the street. I still remember how loud I was screaming with pure joy and excitement. I can say with all certainty, that was the day I was hooked on motorsports. These are my fondest memories, but unfortunately, as I grew older, my father and I would start to grow apart.

My favorite memory though was when I was around nine or ten years old and my father got up to go to work early in the morning. I was on summer break and waited till he left, then went out and grabbed his tool box and proceeded to take apart the new used minibike he had just bought me to replace the old one whose motor I had blown up – I never checked the oil on it until it seized, lesson learned. I had just about finished installing the carburetor back on the new minibike when my dad got home from work and caught me with his wrenches in my hand, while I struggled to screw in the last bolt to the carburetor. By the look on his face, he was not happy at all and started to scold me, reminding me that there was nothing wrong with the new bike. However, very sure of myself, I proceeded to tell him that there was something wrong with the transmission and that was why I had to swap out the bottom end from the spare motor, and install it on the new minibike.

In a very stern voice he told me that after dinner we would take it out and, if the motorcycle would not start, I would be in trouble. Well, although I was very confident that I was right I was too young and ignorant of what could have gone wrong in the swap. I was starting to get concerned that maybe this time, unlike all the other times that I had taken apart the radio, the TV and the VCR—everything else I could get my hands on, I may have gone too far. Right after dinner we took the minibike out to the back yard and to his amazement the darn thing started right up.

But even more shocking was my father taking me along for the ride sitting behind me. Then he shifts it into second gear and the bike no longer has any issues like it had before. I looked back and up at him with a cocky look on my face and he just gave me a little smile that indicated I wasn't in trouble.

And that little bike never let me down. I rode it everywhere and on the weekends my dad would lay it in the back of his station wagon and drop me off (since I wasn't old enough to ride it on the road or on the highway) over the bridge into Fort Myers where my closest friend from school lived. Once there, my buddy Eric and I would struggle to get it unflooded after being laid down on its side on the ride over. But once it started, we would ride all day long deep inside the wooded sugar sand trails that Florida so modestly has to offer. It was hard riding but it made me a better rider learning to ride over that type of terrain. So, when I wasn't trying to break Evel Knievel records on my bicycle, I was either racing or riding my BMX bike or mini bike around with my friends.

It was a great time and a great way to grow up and would always serve me as a way to escape my reality, clear my head and keep me out of trouble. To this day, two-wheel therapy is the best therapy when I need to escape.

Stereotyped

Those first few months in the new school were great, that is, until the day I would meet my Physical Education teacher. That was the day I would learn all about racism and racial profiling. Of course, that's not what it was called back then but it left a mark nonetheless. My P. E. teacher walked up to me and asked me where I was from. "From Colombia, South America," I said.

He responded, "Oh, so your family are drug dealers!"

At the time, I had no idea what he was talking about or what "drug dealer" meant. But the way he looked at me was enough for me to understand that he disliked Colombian people. All the same, on no account was I going to have him disrespect my family.

So I did my best to give him a taste of the angry, resentful little boy that I used to be and gave him a piece of my mind with the most colorful English words I knew. And it must have worked because he ended sending me to see the principal. I was glad that he did, hoping to tell him what the teacher had said to me. However, probably due to lack of communication, or the principal felt the same as the teacher, and I ended up being benched for two weeks every time I went out to P.E. But to me it was all worth it: I wasn't going to let anyone talk bad about my family, ever!

The Ugly Truth

The Good The Bad and The Ugly

Weeks later the most exciting thing happened at school. The school invited the local police to come out and teach us about "illegal drugs," what they were, what they looked like and why they were so bad. They showed us mock samples of cocaine, marijuana and other drugs so we would know what they looked like. They also taught us all about the bad people that were selling them and all the harm they were doing to the people that bought these drugs from them. They told us that, if we ever saw any of these drugs or the bad people, to let them know. I went home that day, so excited about all they had taught us. I was so proud of myself for learning all about this, and I shared it with my parents.

A few weeks after the police presentation at our school, I got home and walked in but no one was around. I looked for my mother and father but could not find either of them. What I did find though would change my life forever. I tried opening the door of our bathroom but it seemed like something on the other side was in the way. I peeked over to see what was keeping the door from opening up all the way and, to my horror, I saw what I never expected.

That was the day I would find out that we were the bad family, the bad people that the police had taught me about earlier in school! My father, my mother, even I—we were the "Bad People." I was in extreme shock. My life had just been turned upside down and would never be the same. It was as if my innocence and my soul had just been ripped right out of me. I was hoping that I was just dreaming and that I would soon wake up; but I knew better. There was no denying what my eyes had just seen. I felt hollow and empty inside as if I had just been gutted open. All this happened in an instance, of course, but it felt at the moment like an eternity. I would never be the same now knowing the truth ... this dirty secret would haunt me for most of my life and would consume my whole youth. I now had to deal with the fact that my family at any moment might be arrested or that the bad drug people that my father worked for might want to kill my father or the whole family.

I quickly closed the door, ran out of the house and went and hid somewhere else. I felt totally different. I instantly felt I had to take charge and help protect my mother and my brother and even my father. If need be from now on, I had to keep this dirty secret hidden in order to protect my father from being arrested. I also knew that I had to start looking over my left shoulder for the bad people who may want to hurt my family and over my right shoulder for the police. I felt it was my responsibility to protect my family and I no longer had time to be a kid. I had to grow up and keep everyone safe.

So, I withdrew and became quiet. I can recall becoming more serious, no longer playful and carelessly laughing as before. I decided I would now act like the man that my family needed me to be to keep them safe. I believe this was the driving force that led me to continue my lifelong journey in the martial arts, always on the alert and ready, though dreading the moment I would need to protect my family. I became more alert and aware of my surroundings and couldn't trust anyone completely, always second guessing their motives for being around me.

Then one day I saw my mother weeping and I asked her what was wrong. She broke down and told me that she was worried about my father because he had not contacted her yet. That was the day she would finally tell me the truth and share the whole story about how my dad got caught up in this whole mess. I also shared with her what I had accidentally discovered.

She told me that my father had always tried to do the right thing but his own family had always dragged him into their dirty affairs. That was, in fact, the reason he had come to the U.S. as he wanted to have a fresh start away from his family. But the day she fell and broke her back, my father had to swallow his pride and ask for their help to pay for all the medical expenses. Once he reached out to them, it opened the door once again for their control and manipulation. They helped with all the hospital expenses but in return they would eventually ask him to set up contacts as well as find a pilot with a twin-engine plane to transport drugs for them into the States. This would not be the first time they had used him and would certainly not be the last.

Just as they requested, he found a pilot, whose name was Gene. Nicest guy and great pilot. For some reason he really enjoyed getting me sick every time he took me up for a ride in his plane, though, somehow, to this day, I still enjoying flying. I was then too young and oblivious of what was really going on during this time, so I really didn't connect all the dots until the day I found all the bags of cocaine on the bathroom floor. But the day my mother and I shared the truth with each other, it all started making sense.

Watching my mother that day in so much pain really tore me apart. It would become another wedge between my father and me. I could not comprehend why my father would allow all of this to happen to our family. Why would he allow this way of life to cause so much pain to my mother? I thought I was tough enough to deal with the truth of my father's lifestyle. But I was helpless, seeing my mother in so much pain and turmoil, not knowing if my father and Gene were still alive or if they had crashed landed somewhere in the ocean on their flight back to Florida, or if the authorities had arrested them, or, even worse, were killed by the cartel. No news, not even a phone call. We had no idea what to think. We were getting increasingly more worried not hearing from them. Seeing my mother like this was tearing me apart with every passing hour. I didn't know what to do or how to make her feel better, I just knew I never wanted to see her in such pain again.

Fortunately, my dad finally called and, to my mother's great relief, he was okay. But I could see that it had taken a toll on her and this would not be the only time lack of news would cause her so much distress.

I found out later the reason my father had asked to borrow my Catholic cross that I wore so faithfully. I always had a strong belief in God, and I always wore it because my dad had given it to me when I was very young and he always saw how much I counted on it to keep us safe. So he asked me if he could borrow it, which I gladly did.

On the flight back from Colombia with the plane full of drugs, they experienced a few close calls. They had taken all the seats out, even the two front ones, so they had to sit on the bales of marijuana the entire trip. In fact, the plane was so loaded down, they almost crashed. Realizing how low their fuel reserves were, they started to look for a place to crash land in the sea. Fortunately, they were flying near Cuba, so they decided to take a chance and land and ask permission to refuel and take off once again.

As they landed, the Cuban military quickly surrounded them. My dad told Gene not to say a word and he would talk to them. Somehow my dad convinced or paid off the military to refuel their plane and let them take off again without incident. This is what delayed their flight back. My mother would later recount to me that my dad held on to that cross with the same belief that I always had in it, and trusted that it would get them back home safely again.

My Mother's Love

My mother was a very beautiful and strong woman, stronger than I imagined. She was my rock and comfort, the only one I could ever talk to about anything including my dreams, and I always made sure she felt the same way. Under that outer beauty was an even more beautiful soul but, through my naïve eyes, I could not see her true inner strength. All I could see was this broken woman, who underneath that facade of composure, was scared, and even mortified of what the future held for the only man she had ever loved. She was totally in love and devoted to this man even though he had many demons and much pain to conquer within.

My father was a complicated man but, through it all, he still shared everything he ever possessed. He had the biggest heart you could ever find in a man of such modest stature and his smile always had such a calming effect on others. His calm composure and modesty were contagious to everyone who met him and his passion for life and smile were enough for my mother to fall hopelessly in love with him and remain devoted to him her whole life. In her eyes he was the most wonderful man she would ever know.

I struggled to accept my father for who he was and the choices that he made because at the time I could not understand his reasoning for what he did. Still, despite all his sins and faults, I loved him truly and still do. But, at the time, all I could see was my mother's constant pain, and the more I witnessed her suffering, the more it would drive a wedge between my father and me. I really tried to overlook his faults but all I could see was the pain he was causing our family, especially my mother: it was almost unforgivable in my eyes. How could a man married to such a beautiful, devoted wife take her for granted? How could he be willing to cause her so much pain and turmoil?

This pain would also extend beyond his business dealings. As I mentioned before, my father was a very unassuming confident alpha male type and the ladies were always attracted to him everywhere he went. To make matters worse, other woman would constantly flirt and throw themselves at my dad right in front of my mother, something I would personally witness my whole life. This would become another reason for the ever-increasing distance between my father and me. It always made me furious and I would constantly have to defend my mother's honor against these women. It seemed my father either didn't care or found it amusing to be showered with such affection by the ladies. Or maybe he felt he had every right to all his conquests because he was a man. Unfortunately, this is very much a part of our culture, and is accepted by many as the norm in my country.

I remember when I first arrived in the U.S. how my father would take me around and show me off like a proud father to all his friends, particularly his very friendly and pretty female friends. At the time I couldn't understand what was going on but I soon began to wise up, and as I got older the rift between us increased with his constant adulterous affairs. They were a slap in the face to my mother. How could he do this to her? I could not understand why he would cheat on my mother at every opportunity he got and, even more confusingly, why would my mother always forgive him? It was beyond me—I just couldn't understand her love and devotion towards this man. I loved them both deeply, but this would always be a constant struggle to understand and a source of turmoil and arguments among us all.

One day, one of his guitar players from the trio he played with at parties and on the local radio station had stayed the night because he was too drunk to make it home. In the morning when he got up, he started to make advances at my mother. With my father at work, he thought it would be a good idea to make his intentions known to her. She didn't appreciate it and quickly called my father at work. He rushed back home and taught this friend a lesson, a lesson that was extremely hard for me to witness as a young boy. I didn't see the confrontation between them, but I could hear it. It was obvious that my dad had been pushed to his limit because his generosity and trust had been broken. It was a traumatizing moment for me as I had never witnessed my father become so enraged. I could hear the strikes landing and the agonizing groans of his friend as he was thrown from one side to the other, never having the chance to say a word.

I witnessed my father turn into a man I did not recognize, a violent man protecting my mother's honor and his. It was a side of him I had never seen before, and it would not be the last time I would witness it. Then, although it was a very violent outburst, it would soon be water under the bridge: they mended their friendship and my father forgave him. This was an example of his big humble heart supplanting his confident alpha male ego and making way for forgiveness.

Missing Him

A Deafening Absence

As I got older, I started to feel more and more of a disconnect with my father to the point that, even though I loved him, I was having a hard time liking him. I grew even more resentful every time he abandoned us, which was becoming more and more frequent. Although I was getting used to it, I could not stand to see my mother so distraught over his frequent and prolonged absences.

At first, he would take off to do a job for his family for a couple of days. But soon a two- or three-day job would turn into a week or two, and eventually into months away from us. I was getting old enough and disengaged enough so that I wouldn't even notice, but soon his absence would start to affect both my mother and brother very badly. I would catch my mother staring out a window into nothingness or trying to cover up the fact that she had been crying. For my brother, on the other hand, it was less noticeable maybe because he was younger and more preoccupied with his activities; but I could tell that it was hurting him as well.

Unfortunately, all of the resentment inside of me and the desire to protect and look after my mother would divide our family. My father would come to choose my brother over me, while my mother would lean on me for support as I did with her. Maybe my father felt betrayed because I would always choose to take her side instead of his: but I had to. I had no choice. No one else would. I had to be her protector, and the one to comfort her each time my father abandoned her.

But being there for my brother was proving to be even more difficult. Maybe one of the reasons for his resentment was because I was to blame for dividing the family and the reason our dad was no longer around, not even for him. Understandably, it wasn't his fault; he wasn't old enough to realize what was really going on and that it wasn't right that our dad was treating our mother the way he was when he was home. Nonetheless, I could see the pain in his young face as he struggled to be brave for my mother and for himself. I wish I knew what to say to him to take away the confusion, the pain and the loneliness that we all felt. But

I did not, not even for myself. All I could do was to be there for them, and for my mother. I would constantly tell her how much I loved her and how beautiful she was, and tried to always be there for her, occasionally surprising her with her favorite flower—a rose. My dad had even planted them all over the garden for her because we all knew how much she loved red roses. They would bloom all around the house and this is how I gave her the nickname "Mi Rosa Linda," "My Beautiful Rose." It was her escape and she seemed the happiest when she was tending to them.

My dad had bought her the house of her dreams and adorned it with her favorite decor on the inside and her favorite flowers on the outside. But he could not give her what she truly desired: his love, time and affection. This was something he could never truly give her and would prove impossible even to the bitter end.

With my father's increasing adulterous affairs I could see the pain of a broken heart in my mother's eyes. Though she would always put on a smile around us and somehow gather up the strength to get dressed and go visit her sister across town, it was evident that she was only a shell of herself—not quite all there, always looking past everyone out into the distance—heart broken.

On one of her visits to her sister's house along with a few other couples that were also invited, all of the sudden no one could find her. She had returned home. When my aunt called her, she explained that she just couldn't bear being there alone, watching all the other married women with their husbands when she had no idea where her husband was or with whom. The light within her was slowly dimming with the continual absence of the only man she ever loved.

But, fortunately, she would come to find comfort in my cousin Sandra. Sandra was her sister Deicy's little girl, and was like my younger baby sister. She was always staying over, and every chance my mother got, she would go pick her up. We all loved having her stay with us and my mother would treat her like her very own. Sandra would come to play a very important role in my mother's life. Maybe she found solace in my cousin because it brought back memories and comfort of the life that could have been with her first child Astrid. Either way, I could see how happy it would always make my mother having her stay with us.

Those two were inseparable at times. My mother would always ask my cousin what she had learned in school that day and my cousin would share all she had been taught especially when it came to astronomy. It was one of their favorite subjects, and so my cousin would jump at the chance to share with her all about it. What a blessing she was to my mother at a time when she most needed someone at her side to distract her from her pain! For that, I am so grateful to my cousin, and for all the precious moments they would get to share together.

In my case, however, with each infidelity, I was becoming more and more resentful towards my father. I could not stand seeing my mother suffer so much. This once strong courageous woman was literally falling apart before my eyes, and I could do nothing to help her. Even our relationship was becoming fragile. My only solution for her was to persuade her to divorce my father but I could see in her eyes that this was something unimaginable. I could not understand why she wouldn't snap out of it and regain her dignity and peace of mind. To me, it was a simple solution to ending her pain and starting a new life with someone new that would appreciate and love her as she deserved. We argued many times about it but she would rather accept the pain and humiliation of loving my father than being without him. At the time I could not understand this kind of love, which was beyond anything I had ever witnessed. I knew that all she needed was someone that would truly make her happy once again. I know my father loved her once because of all the stories I had heard about how he would serenade her declaring his love for her. But the name "Dágo" does mean to supplant to conquer ... was this all my mother was to him—just another conquest among his trophies? I would hate to think so. I do believe that they were once happy.

But all this turmoil was tearing us apart to our detriment. One day when my mother was away in Colombia visiting her family, while my brother and I stayed behind, my father showed up after a very long absence. It was maybe a couple of years or more since we had last seen or heard from him. This was the longest time he had been away, without even contacting any one of us, especially my brother, so it was unusual. It was almost strange to see him back but that night he seemed very agitated and angry. A verbal confrontation would ensue.

The last time we had gotten into an argument was the time I stepped in to stop a fight between my mother and him. He used to get more and more agitated and violent at home maybe due to the stress he was dealing with in that world. Or maybe it was us that were demanding something from him that he did not know or want to give: his love, his time or attention. One night the argument would become physical, and I stepped in to save my mom, and that's when things really changed between us. I ended up with a broken nose after thinking I was old enough to hold my own against him; but I was gravely mistaken.

This time, though, with my brother and me alone with him, it was different. Although it didn't end up in a physical confrontation, it almost ended very tragically when a gun was introduced. Thank God neither of us had any intention of using it; but it showed the enormous stress he was obviously under and how out of hand our relationship had gotten. I was heartbroken and shocked to think he believed that I—his own son—would be willing to take his life.

This was a cry for help from him but at the time I did not understand what he was going through. What was happening? We hadn't seen him in a couple of years and now this tragedy almost takes place. Something was greatly amiss, and I did not know at the time what it was exactly. But that was all soon to change.

Shortly after my mother returned from Colombia, she and my father immediately flew back to

Colombia. Meanwhile, my brother and I stayed behind with our aunt Deicy dropping by to keep an eye on us. As teenagers we would continue in our everyday routine—my brother would go to school and I would continue to train for my cycling events. My mother and I had agreed that I would take a year off to pursue a professional cycling career before enrolling at the local college. In the meantime, my brother and I started to notice some strange things happening around us, which were becoming increasingly obvious.

The last time I had noticed something strange was going on was the time my father's cousin came to live with us for a whole summer. What was strange was that he never left our side—not even to the bathroom—and my brother and I were not allowed to go outside that entire summer. At the time we really didn't think much about it and why my mother and father were not around that whole summer. But, eventually, once I got old enough, my mother would explain to me that my father's side of the family had placed a price on me and my brother's head until my father paid back a huge part of a shipment of money that had allegedly gone missing. Strangely enough, this would happen every time my father would tell his family this was his last job for them.

This time, though, things felt entirely different as was evident by the undercover cars that kept following us everywhere we went.

Naked and Exposed

One humid summer night two individuals knocked at the door that led to the house from the garage. I answered and, to my amazement, it was someone I remembered, our old neighbor. Turns out he was the son of a local sheriff at the time that use to live right next door to us and now he was at my door with a strange woman, who wasn't his wife. They both started to ask where my father was and when I had last seen him. If only they hadn't been so obvious about wearing their matching "Members Only" jackets in the middle of a hot humid summer night, I may have been more inclined to share what I did or did not know.

They obviously saw I wasn't going to share much with them, maybe because I couldn't keep my eyes off of their stylish summer jackets, wondering what kind of recording devices they may have been hiding under them. I wasn't about to help someone that had always pretended to like us and be a friend of my father, who was now trying to squeeze information out of me about him. I'd never trusted him and his fake friendly demeanor, and this just wasn't going to happen. I always felt he was up to something, always looking out for himself and that night was confirmation.

The next few days were even stranger seeing all these people hanging around this white telephone work van right next to our dear neighbor's house. It was just odd to see so many telephone line workers dressed in business suits hiding behind a van eyeing our every move when my brother and I would leave or come back to the house. And more obvious was the constant following of all of us as we drove around town. Everywhere we went, a standard undercover cop car with its cheap shiny chrome hub caps, carrying one or two individuals in business suits would be tailing us. We had all seen them, even my mother once she got back from Colombia. It was so obvious that I never even worried that it may be the cartel looking to kidnap or kill us because, even though I was somewhat ignorant about that world, I knew from watching all those famous mob movies like Scar Face that you might never see the mob come get you, you could not say the same about the sophistication of the local police or even the FBI.

Alejandro's Allegation

Maybe I had become too complacent or was just consumed with being a teenager and having a girlfriend that I really didn't give it too much thought. Until one afternoon as I was watching TV when I got a call from one of my father's former shop employees Alejandro. My father had a local paint and body shop with two other partners before he decided to run off to California with another woman, accompanied by his shop manager Alejandro. My father had been warned that Alejandro would someday get him into trouble because he was so wild and unpredictable. One day he stole my dad's wagon to get his fix and showed up the next day with my dad's station wagon all shot up. That was the kind of person he was. However, my dad had a soft spot for him because as a young boy Alejandro had tragically witnessed his father's plane crash, and so my dad always tried to mentor and became a kind of father figure to him.

On that day Alejandro called and I answered. He told me that he was in town and wanted to stop by and buy my old go kart to take back to Ecuador for his younger brother. I told him I would sell it and we agreed that he would stop by later that evening. So I sat back down and continued to watch TV when the local news interrupted with a live newsflash about a suspect they were following walking into the local mall. And while I'm watching the live breaking news I could see them arrest the person; but it never registered that the man they had just arrested on live TV was actually Alejandro. It would not sink in until later on that evening when we received a call from the local newspaper and the reporter asked my brother what he thought about his father being a wanted drug kingpin and a suspect in a murder investigation.

My brother, barely sixteen then, turned to me and asked what the hell he was talking about. It was a total shock for my brother to find out about the family secret this way. He had always been spared the paranoia of having to deal with the truth of our father's business dealings. In a single instant, his world and the image of the man he so loved and admired came crumbling down. It pained me to watch what he was having to experience. I grabbed the phone and told the journalist to go to hell and hung up.

I then tried to calm my brother down as best I could. We got out of the house and took a ride to go talk, and I proceeded to tell him the whole truth. I owed it to him. I needed to finally be honest with him. I couldn't shield him from the family secret any longer. This was very painful for me to have to do especially under the circumstances. As I had mentioned before, my mother had already returned from Colombia and that very evening she briefly told me what was happening. But I would never quite be ready for what we were about to experience because things were going to change drastically from that moment on.

The Bad Family

The next morning my mother goes out and returns with the local paper and hands it to me. I read the headlines, "Dágoberto Drug Kingpin wanted as suspect in a murder investigation." I was beside myself. Not only had our worst fears come true but the worst possible things were being said about my father. And now the family secret was out there for the whole world to see. The bad family was finally exposed, while everyone else was proven right. All the racial profiling of my family and all the times I had defended my nationality, and my family were now proven to be unjustified. There was no more denying it, no more hiding from the truth; the light had finally exposed our dirty dark family secret.

But most painful and shocking were the allegations of murder and claims of my father being a "kingpin." From what I had been told by my mother, my father's dealings were based on him being the little guy caught in the middle of his family's dealings. Of course, understandably, news like this coming out of a small southern town would most likely need to be sensationalized especially during the local elections. Case in point, was one of my dad's close acquaintances, a police officer and long-time customer of my dad's paint and body shop, who, coincidentally and conveniently, never ended up paying for services at the shop. Nevertheless, he still had enough credibility to tell the newspapers and local TV stations how he had been watching my father for a very long time and knew that he was a kingpin; somehow, he wouldn't say why he had never acted before this to try and arrest him. However, now in the middle of his campaign to run for sheriff, my father's story was front and center every morning and evening for the next two weeks, while he garnered votes for his election.

Yes, I was angry and I get it: my father was just a stepping stone to his political ends and, yes, my father had made his own bed. But at the same time, it felt so hypocritical and unfair to profit off, what I believed at the time, was unfair and cruel publicity for his own gain. I was angered watching all this unfold right before our eyes and for all of us to be judged in the court of public opinion without first being given our constitutional right of being innocent until proven guilty. I was angry not so much about what was being said about my father but what it was doing to my mother and my brother—how much this was affecting them.

As it turns out, when my father left my mother for the final time, the reason for his long absence was another woman. This was not uncommon for my father but his decision to be with this woman would be his downfall and the reason for his destruction as a man and the destruction and loss of everything he had and loved.

Despite being blessed with a loving and devoted wife that had given him three children, my father still chose to chase and lust after forbidden fruits. He had also been blessed with making it out alive after serving in Colombia's civil war and had been given the grace to start a new life, an honest life, in America. But he chose to throw it all away. Maybe he never believed he could lose it all and thus never saw it slipping away. Or maybe he was blinded by his lust and stubborn bravado. Maybe he just couldn't help but to live up to his given name of "Dágo" That's perhaps why he fell victim to the age-old temptation of sex, money and power. I truly can't say; only God knows the truth. Nevertheless, to me, the father I knew was not a murderer. He wasn't perfect either—just a sinner in God's eyes like the rest of us. Regardless, what he had set into motion would be the beginning of his downfall—his adulterous affairs and dark secret would finally catch up on him.

CHAPTER 7

The Escape

A Sacrificial Love

A few minutes after my mother arrived with the newspaper story about my father, the house was surrounded by both local police and the FBI. As they entered our home, my brother and I noticed that a few of them were the same ones that had been stalking us for weeks beforehand. My brother said to one of them," I know you. You're that guy that keeps following me around everywhere I go." The agent got beat red and visibly upset but denied it was him. It was obvious this was a jab at them from my brother; he was upset and wanted them to know it.

We were then taken to a separate part of the house and questioned individually as to the whereabouts of my father. We each said the same thing: that after the separation of my mother and father we hadn't seen him for over two years. To us that was the truth, because the night my brother and I had the confrontation with him, he was not the man we used to know; he was different—something had changed in him. But we weren't going to tell them anything: he was still our father and that's where our loyalty stood.

After the initial shock of what had just happened we were left feeling like a Mac truck had just plowed right into the side of us. We were left confused, stunned and not sure what was going to happen to us or my father.

The story was later told to me by my mother about what had happened in California. However, it did not make any sense to either one of us because the man that had lost his life was an associate and close friend of my father's. My mother had known him and his family and they were both very fond of him and his wife. Although I had never met them, I had heard all about them and what a beautiful family they had! I remember my parents talking very fondly about them, so to me it would be unthinkable to believe the allegations that Alejandro had made to the police and the newspapers after he was arrested; it just did not make any sense. Alejandro stated that my father told him to kidnap his associate and hold him for ransom until his wife paid for his release. I started filling in what may have happened and, knowing Alejandro and what kind of lifestyle he led, it would slowly begin to make more sense. Now I am not trying to make excuses for either my father or Alejandro as I wasn't there to know what actually happened, but after hearing my mother's side of the story and eventually a few others,' I would slowly start to piece things together.

According to my mother, Alejandro had reached out to her and said that my father was depressed and lost in a dark place and needed to see her. So my mother flew out to California to see my father and that's when my father would tell her what had happened. It seems that one day my father came home to find Alejandro sleeping with his mistress, and this enraged him to the point of beating Alejandro and kicking him out of the house. With no place to go and a bad drug habit, Alejandro may have decided to go kidnap my father's associate and hold him for ransom while going on a three-day drug binge, leaving my dad's friend inside the trunk of a car. After a few days, he went to return him to his wife and pick up the ransom money and, as he opened the trunk to get him out, he realized that the man had passed away either from dehydration or from the heat. Panicking, he left the car with the body and returned to my father asking for forgiveness and help. But it was too late now, a friend and associate had just died.

The FBI told us that Alejandro had told the man's wife that he had been sent by my father to kidnap her husband. They also believed that his death may have been unintentional. Either way, Alejandro had implicated my father as the mastermind behind the kidnapping. I don't know. I never asked my father the truth of what had actually occurred but, in my mind, the only thing that made sense to me was that Alejandro was possibly implicating my father as revenge for having been caught with his mistress and beaten. I may never know or want to know the truth of what may have led to such a tragic end for this man and his family. But somehow, I felt we were all to blame for living in that world, a world I can never detest enough for giving and taking everything we ever had. It had always felt like we were all living a cursed life, never a peaceful second, always looking over our shoulder watching to see if our sins were ever going to catch up to us.

My father must have been feeling the same guilt and remorse. He was beside himself, not knowing what to do, and started to slip into a dark state of depression. I now realize why the night of that confrontation with my brother and me, he had acted like a man without any hope or reason to live. The consequences of his actions and his faith and trust in the wrong people had ultimately caught up with him, and this time there was no way out ... or so it would seem.

Risking it All for the Man She Loved

My mother flew to California to talk with my father and see what he wanted. I can only imagine that the truth was far from what she was hoping to hear from him. I believe she still clung to some sort of hope that my father would come to his senses and decide to come back home to her and leave that life and the woman he was with behind. Unfortunately, she was wrong. That ugly, horrible life was far from over. Many times he had promised her that this would be the last time; but now it wasn't so much at the hands of his family who would always force him back in as his own doing. His downfall would come from his own choices, and his one last time had just become his undoing.

What we sow, we reap:

*For he that soweth to his flesh shall of the flesh
reap corruption; but he that soweth to the Spirit shall
of the Spirit reap life everlasting* (Galatians 6:8).

Once my mother had heard the tragic truth of what
had happened, she was devastated. She felt used and
lied to about why my dad wanted to see her again;
but the love that she felt for this man was still too
strong for her to turn her back on him now. And so
she decided to drive all the way back to Florida with
my father. Once back home, she came up with a way
to get him out of the country. It was a very simple but
unfathomable plan to get my father on a plane without his passport; he would claim to U.S. Immigration
on leaving that he had lost his passport and IDs, and
desperately needed to attend his mother's funeral
in Colombia. The same story would be told to the
Colombian authorities upon landing. It was the risk-
iest and most desperate plan ever imagined ... but
somehow it worked.

My father was able to fly into Colombia undetected
all because of the sheer power of love and determination to keep the love of her life alive and out of
jail. They both feared that my father would never
get a fair trial in the States. Being Colombian was
strike one because of the well-deserved reputation

that so many had inflicted upon our country. And strike two was the difficulty in presenting his case due to the language barrier. Up until then, I had been their interpreter anytime they needed me. However, this time it would not suffice and the decision to go on the run was made. And it would be the beginning of his downfall.

Her Fight to Live

My mother's fight for life would not come at the hands of a vengeful cartel or by the hand of justice for helping my father escape to Colombia. Her fight would be against time. We take many things in life for granted, and most of all, our God-given time with one another. It's the only thing we can never have enough of and once gone never get back.

The time right after the FBI and local police descended on our house, my mother was barely sleeping and not eating enough. She was surviving on only a couple hours of sleep at the most and consuming mostly coffee and the occasional snack. She was too saddened about what had happened to the family and the man she loved so dearly. I can only imagine what must have been going through her mind about the potential loss of the man she loved and the loss of a father for her children. This constant worry about my father's whereabouts must have been what was consuming her every thought. All this would start to take a toll on her health.

Nonetheless, she would continue to put on a brave face for my brother and me amidst the constant barrage of newspaper articles and nightly news reports of the allegations against my father.

That old saying, "You learn who your true friends really are in tough times" would become very evident during these times. Aside from my aunt Deicy and her husband Mike, my cousin Sandra and our cousins Fabio and Margarita who have always been there through thick and thin and my mother's dear friend Nellie all but one other family friend Mariela, the encyclopedia sales lady, no one else would stand by my mother's side. All the other so-called friends would show their true colors and avoid us at all costs. Only a few friends of my brother would continue to show their support, but none of the ones I considered my closest of friends wanted to be associated with us. In their minds, we must have been like the plague. My brother would have such a rough time that he had to leave school because of the constant harassment for being the son of a so-called "KingPin." Ironically, it wasn't even coming from the other students but from the teachers, particularly the shop teacher who I liked very much and considered a good person. So, it was very disheartening and sad to hear that the bullying was actually coming from him, an adult who should have acted more responsibly.

Only a couple of my brother's friends from high school would still come around, especially one who was like a brother to us, Brent. I can never thank him enough for not turning his back on my brother. I couldn't say the same about my own friends, though, but I really couldn't blame any of them. It was our bed; we had made it, and now we were living the consequences of our dark secret.

One evening while a couple of my brother's friends were hanging out at the house, my mother comes into the kitchen to grab some grapes to snack on and, as she ate one, she started to choke. Once I realized she was choking, I quickly began to perform the Heimlich maneuver. But no matter how hard I tried, the grape would not come out. By this time my mother was starting to turn blue and I was starting to get very worried. Fortunately, my brother's really strong friend Mark grabbed my mother, properly performed the Heimlich maneuver and was able to get the grape to come out. We were all relieved but this close call only foreshadowed the things to come.

The next day my mother, feeling a little sore from the previous night, mentioned something that seemed very strange. She said that she felt like something had ruptured and felt a cold liquid running all over inside of her. Neither of us could figure out what this actually might have been but we brushed it off as nothing to be concerned about. Besides, we were both just thankful that she was all right now since it had been such a scary situation.

Months passed and we started noticing her belly growing to the point that she made a joke that maybe she was pregnant again. We found it humorous and, once again, we would brush it off. But her tummy would continue to grow larger, and we both started getting concerned. Months earlier she had been seen by her OB/GYN doctor and had received a clean bill of health, so she wasn't really concerned until the pains started and then continued to get worse. I then noticed a change in her demeanor. I could see in her eyes how this was adding to her stress. But she would always put on a brave face and refuse to go see another doctor. Regardless of her condition, she would continue with her plans to move back home to Bogota, although she would quickly find herself in a place she feared the most.

Home to Retire

Her original plan, before everything unfolded with my father, was to move back home to Colombia to be close to her family once again. My brother and I were now old enough to be on our own and looking for our own apartment. She was coming to grips with my father no longer being in our lives, and finally looking forward to starting a new life without him. I believe we were all finally getting used to the idea of life without him.

After things calmed down a bit at the home front with the FBI seemingly not surveilling us so closely, they gave us some breathing room, probably hoping that we would lead them straight to my father. Unfortunately, by this time no one in our family knew his whereabouts and so my mother continued with her original plan of moving back home to live close to her family. But time was catching up and soon we would all find out just how little time we had.

Succumbing to the Pain, 1987

Soon after arriving in Bogota in late August—literally the very next day—my mother experienced such excruciating pain from her belly that it knocked her out. She was rushed to the hospital where she woke listening to the doctors tell her and the family that she had a cancerous tumor in her ovaries that had ruptured and spread to all her lower organs and was making its way up to her heart. They needed to operate immediately to cut it out and clean as much as they could to try and stop the spread to the rest of her organs.

My brother and I were not privy to this discussion, and we didn't arrive until right before they prepped her for surgery. But I do recall about halfway into the eight-hour surgery seeing the main surgeon come out and talk to my uncle's wife Beatrice. As I watched them from afar, they both looked over at me as if in slow motion, or so it seemed, and then the doctor got called and turned and rushed back.

I sensed that something was not right and being raised a Catholic, I quickly sought out the hospital chapel and fell to my knees, crying out to God with every ounce of faith I could muster. I asked God in my heart, "Please give me one more Christmas and one more Mother's Day with my mother—that's all I ask." I was crying uncontrollably when my two cousins Madeleine and Sasa found me. They tried to comfort me, but I could not be reached, lost in a vastness of pain. I did not know exactly what was happening but I could tell that something was not right by the look on my aunt's and the doctor's face.

Four hours later the doctor returns to the waiting room to talk to the family. I approached the doctor as he was talking to my aunts and uncles, and I would come to realize the gravity of the situation and learn about her illness for the first time. The doctor explained that the cancerous tumor had been successfully removed and cleaned up as much as they could, but he believed that she had very little time left—only a few months at the most because of how aggressive the cancer was.

My Earnest Prayer

After three days in intensive care, my mother came to and asked to see me. I was the first to see her and, as I approached, she reached out and grabbed my hand, gently and lovingly caressing it. While looking into my eyes; she told me that she had never seen me cry so much before. In the moment I was thinking she was recalling a time when I was a little boy and had fallen down crying but that's not what she was referring to. She continued to tell me that she saw me in the small chapel crying uncontrollably, asking

God to save her and then she saw my two cousins come in and try to console me. Then she told me that she saw the whole family, all her sisters and brothers and my grandmother, sitting in the waiting room waiting for any news. She then continued to tell me that the reason she had seen all this was because she had risen above her body and watched while all the doctors gave up trying to resuscitate her—all but one. It was the anesthesiologist, who stayed and continued trying to revive her along with his assistant. And as she's sharing this with me, a man enters her room and she looks up at him and says, "I know you!"

He answers, "You do?"

My mother replies, "Yes, you're the doctor that saved my life," and he humbly smiled back at her as if confirming he was the anesthesiologist.

You see, the doctor I'd seen come out of surgery four hours into her surgery was the main surgeon coming out to tell the family they had lost her. The doctors had already declared her clinically dead for more than ten minutes. But, thanks to the efforts of that one humble and persistent doctor that kept pumping on her heart even after everyone else had walked out, she was revived. And during these ten minutes of being clinically dead is when she saw her family and me in the chapel.

She also mentioned seeing a bright light coming from a tunnel and described the moment as being very peaceful and devoid of any pain. Within it, she saw her beloved grandmother Isabela along with Saint Gregorio, a doctor she was deeply devout to, reaching out to her and telling her that she had suffered long enough and it was time to come home. My mother said that she felt so much peace and love that she wanted nothing more than to go with them and as she moved upward into the light tightly held by her grandmother, she started to think about my brother and me and thought to herself that she hadn't prepared anything for us, and that she couldn't leave us just yet. And so she fought with all her might to break loose and then found herself back in her body. Once she awoke, she couldn't wait to share with me what she had experienced.

Now I know we've all heard many accounts from doctors explaining how the white light is just a manifestation of a brain going through spasms at the very end. Up until that moment, I had always agreed with that theory. But how can you explain how my mother was not only able to see her own body and all her family exactly as we all were in the waiting room and me in the chapel crying and hearing what I was mentally asking God—to allow me to have one more Christmas and one more Mother's Day with her? That to me is not a function of spasms in the brain but it's something far beyond what our small finite minds can comprehend.

Hope For Recovery

Once back home at my grandmother's, we were all attentive to her, making sure that she had every possible need met. We all had high hopes that a miracle would save her, that she was not doomed to the short time predicted by her doctor. So, we all continued to make her as comfortable and happy for as long as we could. This was our unspoken pledge to one another.

My mother was the kind of woman that always carried herself with tremendous dignity and respect. In my eyes she had always been the perfect wife to my father and a loving mother to my brother and me, raising us to be polite and respectful men. Yet I had foolishly judged her to be a weak woman, lacking in confidence because she never stood up for herself against my father. Somehow, although she would always command respect every time she entered a room, she never seemed to receive it from my father. But here I stand decades later realizing how wrong I had been about my mother and how she is still teaching me how to be a better man. Her courage and strength would not come from walking away from all the pain she was being caused but by confronting it and holding on with every fragment of hope even to the bitter end.

I now understand that to her, a life worth living was living a vulnerable life filled with faith, love and hope for something. This was true courage and strength and was to be her greatest lesson to me.

Reunited

Sometime later, my aunt Beatrice bumped into my father and told him that my mother had cancer and did not have much time left and that she had asked to see him. He, on the other hand, ignorantly attributed it to my mother's jealousy of the new woman in his life saying that he never knew that jealousy could cause cancer. I am not sure why he could be so dismissive about my mother's plight even if they did leave on bad terms. But later my uncle Omar met with him and told him that it was true; she was dying of cancer and had very little time left. It may have been a sobering moment for him to finally realize that it was not an exaggeration or ploy by my mother to try and get him back. And so, after reflecting on it, he asked if he could see her.

I remember the night that my father showed up. When she was told that he was there to see her, she asked her sisters to help her sit up and get ready. By now she had become very frail losing all her hair and more than half her weight along with her voice due to the chemotherapy. She could hardly talk, her voice was only a whisper but she summoned the strength to sit up and had one of my aunts get her a scarf to cover her bald little head.

As my father started to walk up the stairs, I noticed that my mother had a totally different demeanor about her. This time I would not see the excited, devoted loving wife that had always awaited his return with open arms and a broken heart. What I saw was a very different woman that was about to make amends with her past. She looked at peace and free from any emotion, without the baggage that had always dragged her down. She was ready to forgive and accept her impending end.

My father entered her room and they both smiled at each other, and I could see my dad's eyes start to water up. Seeing her this way for the first time must have been gut wrenching for him. He walked up to her and kneeled down by her bed and they began to talk. I would come up to check on her from time to time trying to respect their time alone and, every time I did, I noticed my dad breaking down ever so slowly. His hard demeanor was crumbling with every soft-spoken word from my mother. I wasn't privy to their conversation; but I could see that it was a very tender and loving exchange and at one point it seemed as if my father had fallen from the highest of peaks and had come crashing down. I had never seen him so vulnerable, so spent, so totally and utterly enveloped by my mother's love for him. Even then, after all he had ever done, emotionally, physically and mentally to her, he was experiencing the mercy of her love, her forgiveness and her devotion to him, something that he always knew and never doubted. But this would be a defining moment of their love for one another.

After my father left that night, I could see a tremendous sense of peace and calm come over my mother. She had expended all the love and emotion she'd ever had for my father and had gifted it to him one final time. There was a sense of peace now that I had never seen in her before. This would be the peace she had always thirsted for alongside my father.

My father, on the other hand, seemed but a shell of the man that had walked up those stairs. Although he was an alpha male of great courage with a stoic disposition, that night he walked out looking like his soul had been gutted out, as if his life had just passed before his eyes. Walking back down the stairs took every bit of strength from him. He looked empty, spent and broken hearted. Did he just realize he would forever be losing the only woman in his life that truly loved him? Did he realize he had taken her love for granted and would forever lose it? I can only imagine his pain as he walked down those stairs that somber night.

A New Hope

My mother would slowly begin to regain her strength and her hair would start to grow back. This would spark a new hope in all of us especially my mother. We were all starting to feel like maybe there could be a second chance for her, finally a chance at a happy new life.

However, as Christmas approached, unfortunately, she would slowly start to slip back into another low. This time it didn't look like there was much, if any, hope to hold onto anymore. On Christmas Eve we called a Catholic priest to perform the last rites. As he left right before midnight, she gathered her last remaining strength and, to our amazement, sat up and asked to see all her nieces and nephews and as they came up, she pulled out a gift for each of them. This is customary in most Latin countries where we celebrate and exchange gifts on Christmas Eve at midnight. As they all went back down, she turned to the nurse and told her to take her off the morphine drip because she wouldn't be needing it any longer. The nurse did as she requested, and my mother lay back down and went to sleep. The whole night we were all patiently waiting to hear the nurse announce that she had taken her last breath, but it never came. In the morning, she awoke with an added vigor and new life in her eyes. We couldn't believe what we were witnessing. It was a miracle, as if she had been given another chance at finally having that happy life we all wished for her. But this hope would be short-lived and after a few months there would come the catalyst to her final surrender.

Surrendering

We were all starting to feel the stresses from the highs and lows, some more than others. On this particular morning an argument escalated between my mother and one of her sisters to the point where some very harsh words were said to my mother. This was hurtful enough to cause a change in my mother's outlook and state of mind and would be the catalyst to my mother giving up. She was hurt and no longer wanted to be a burden to her sister. I believe it broke her spirit and her will to keep on fighting. I have since been able to forgive this aunts behavior understanding that none of us are perfect and we were all just under tremendous stress. Nonetheless, immediately after the incident my mother asked to go stay with her sister Amparo, who so graciously and eagerly received her. This would be where she was to spend her remaining days.

A Place of Peace and Love

My aunt Amparo did everything to make her happy; there was nothing that she and my uncle Hernando as well as my three dear cousins; Diego, Pacho and Laura would not do for her. My mother felt at peace and very happy with them and I was so grateful for their love and selfless attention for her. I visited her every day and tried to be by her side every minute that I could. Whether this was a conscience decision or not, I did not want to regret not cherishing what little time I had left with her. At the time it was the only thing I lived for every time I woke up and I always looked forward to seeing her smiling face each new day.

Her time with her sister Amparo would be a happy joyful time, peaceful and full of love but her health would still be touch and go, even though she had such a promising turnaround just a few months before. Some days were better than others but, overall, we could see her slow decline and we could all sense the inevitable. It was hard watching her struggle, going through her ups and downs, her promising days being swept away by the bad ones. It was hard for us to watch but even harder for her to go through. I just wish I could have somehow taken all her pain and discomfort away. She didn't deserve this. She was a good woman and the best mother I could have ever asked for.

Yes, we had our differences because of how much she loved my father and would not let him go, but it was now very apparent that it was no longer the case. After their final goodbye, I could sense something different about her. She was no longer broken hearted over my father; she seemed at peace even with what she was going through. I could see a new-found strength and courage in her that I had never seen before and, although comforting, it was also telling of the decision she had already made.

As that fateful day approached, we all braced ourselves for our final goodbyes. It was becoming apparent with each passing day that she had already accepted her fate and knew that her final days were fast approaching and, to be honest, seeing her struggle and in so much pain made me aware that I was just being selfish wanting her to keep on fighting.

Her doctor arrived to check on her once again and he would tell us that there was nothing else he could do for her. He could take her back to the hospital, and maybe keep her alive for another week or so, or we could just let her spend her last remaining days at home. Either way, there was nothing more that could be done. The doctor asked the family what we wanted to do and the family all turned to me and asked for me to make the decision. This would be the hardest decision I would ever have to make. How could I choose between more time with my mother and not causing her anymore pain when every second with her mattered so much to me? Did I not want to let her go for my own selfish reasons? Should I let her go so she could finally rest in peace? It would not take me long to make the right decision. I would choose to let go of my selfishness and have her stay at home and spend her last couple of days in peace and in the comfort and love of her family.

I knew that's what she would want. She never wanted to go back into the hospital, to die in a cold strange place away from all her loved ones. No, she would want to be in a warm, comforting and loving place surrounded by all the people she knew and loved. Even so, I still doubted myself. Was my decision still a selfish one? Had I just decided this because I could no longer stand to see her suffer? But, ultimately, I knew I could not put her through any more pain, not even if it was for my own selfish reasons.

Salvation is Nigh

My uncle Leonidas, an Evangelical Christian, came to see her and spent a good amount of time talking with my mother and sharing the bible with her. Afterwards, he came down the stairs singing and praising the Lord and told us, "She is now ready. She has accepted the Lord and Savior Jesus into her heart." At the time I didn't understand what it actually meant but it was comforting to hear because we all knew him as a great man of God with a joyful smile in his heart, always living the bible, not just preaching it.

That evening the mood became increasingly somber as we all knew what was to come. The whole family had gathered and even my father had come to be by her side in her final hours. Then that dreaded moment came and my aunt Deicy announced to the whole family that she had taken her last breath. I rushed back in and grabbed my mother and laid her head across my lap letting out the most painful scream I'd ever heard come out of me. I had just lost my mother, the only person to really accept me as I was, the only one that never belittled me, the only one to ever believe in me and all my hopes and dreams. She was truly the only person to have ever understood me and now she had just left me. Although I was twenty-two years old, I felt totally abandoned because there would never be anyone else to fill this void in my heart. In that moment I started to reminisce and explain to everyone what a wonderful mother she had been and what she will always mean to me. I was uncontrollably crying and, as I looked back down to see her lovely little face, I noticed a slight smile as she looked back up at me. Maybe it was just my imagination or maybe it was her truly smiling back at me, but I will always take comfort in remembering that last smile. And, as I looked into her eyes feeling that familiar emptiness I'd always felt as a little boy creeping back in, I couldn't help but to feel afraid that all that pain and abandonment would once again return.

But it didn't. On the contrary, in that very instance, I felt this warm embrace enveloping my heart, filling every cell of it with pure unconditional love, and I knew right then that her love would always be with me. No matter where I went and what I did, I would never feel that cold empty void again. This was her final gift to me.

I reached down and gently closed her eyes and, after I laid her back down again, the nurse checked for any vitals and declared my mother deceased. Even though I had been preparing myself for this very moment, now that it was finally here, I was numb. I felt like a part of me had literally been ripped away and I would never love or miss anyone like this ever again.

Farewell

Days prior, my mother had asked her sister Deicy to take care of us and watch over us like her own. She had also instructed her on what to do for the funeral proceedings and what dress and perfume she wanted to be buried in; her favorite had always been an elegant satin chiffon dress. My aunt, wanting to fulfill her wishes and not let anyone else pick her body up and dress her herself, asked me to give her a hand placing my mother's body into the casket after she had finished dressing her. I lovingly obliged.

The last thing I can recall from that night was seeing men coming up the stairs with a casket to pick up my mother's body. It was customary in Colombia to immediately bury our deceased and, with an emptiness, I watched as they carried my mother's body back down the stairs and away to the morgue.

The Burial

The next morning my brother and I were taken by a dear friend of the family to go get our suits for my mother's funeral. My mother had told me that she wanted my brother and me to wear all white at her funeral. She wanted it to be a happy occasion and she did not want us to cry but only remember her being happy, vivacious and courageous. I agreed to honor her wishes. Little did I know how prophetic those words would be.

We were running late, so we hurried back home to my aunt Amparo's house and as we ran into shower and get dressed my aunt kept telling us to hurry. I remember jumping into the shower, and as I washed up I literally heard—no not heard, the best way I can describe it is—I saw a voice behind my right ear telling me to "Hurry up, Chato," which means "Short Nose." That was her endearing nickname for me. At that same moment, crazy and bizarre as this may sound, I know felt my mother's touch spanking my bottom as she said this to me. Undeniable as our mother's touch is when alive, so was hearing and feeling my mother's touch in that moment. That is the best way I can describe what I heard and felt and it didn't scare me: on the contrary, it comforted me. As my brother and I hurried to the funeral home, what we witnessed as we arrived was nothing short of astonishing.

Such Love for My Mother

I couldn't believe my eyes, the number of people, family and friends that made it to her funeral. Some had come from hours away just to pay their respects to this woman that had impacted so many lives with her good deeds and show of affection. I always knew how special she was to others—she truly had a beautiful gentle soul and always treated everyone with love and respect. But I was flabbergasted once I saw the enormity of the crowd that had come out to pay their final respects to my mother. I can never say thank you enough to all of them, every single friend, family member and even strangers that I had never seen before that came up to me and paid their respects, many sharing stories with me of how generous my mother was and how much they loved her. It was very comforting to hear and to have them there. It touched me beyond words.

Once all the burial proceedings were over and they started to lower my mother's casket, her favorite trio started to play one of her three special songs "Merceditas," originally by the group Los Visconti. This song would always be requested by her at all our family gatherings—only this time it was for the final time. In her honor they had changed the name of the broken-hearted girl in the song to my mother's name "Margarita."

As they started to lower my mother's casket, I suddenly found myself floating in this peaceful vastness filled with moving images of my mother and me. I could see myself reliving every single moment of our lives together but, in reverse, moving from that very moment of watching her casket being raised back up to the moment of her last breath in my arms, all the way to when I was a little boy in her arms to the moment of my birth and being in her womb. It was a replay of the most cherished moments of our lives together, and I did not want it to end. I was being gifted with all the moments I could not remember as a child; all the love, the caring and the affection of my mother. But, this celestial place I had found myself in slowly began to fade away and I started to come back into the reality of where I was. I noticed that I had the biggest smile of contentment on my face and, as I looked around, I quickly realized that I was the only one not crying. All my family were crying deeply. As I turned to my brother and father, I could see the loss and pain in their eyes as well, though I caught myself still smiling, and had to force myself to stop in fear of them thinking I had lost my mind.

I remember walking away leaving my mother buried in that casket in the ground, but I no longer felt sad. I only felt a sense of peace and this strange comfort of somehow knowing she was in a better place.

My uncle Hernando, who was always like a father to me ever sense I was a little boy, took me out to eat on our way back home. I could tell he was just concerned and trying to get a feel of where I was mentally and emotionally. In reality, I felt like I was in a good place. For the first time in my life, I felt complete and void of the emptiness and loneliness I had always felt as a little boy not remembering my parents, and the pain that I always carried with me even after being reunited with them in the U.S. Suddenly, it all went away the moment my mother took her last breath. I felt like I could go anywhere and do anything without that nagging emptiness or the fear of failure or not being good enough. It was strange; I couldn't really explain it, not even to myself. That's probably why I wasn't saying much during the meal with my uncle.

So when we got home, I changed and took off for a long walk around the city by myself trying to air out my head and to make sense of everything I was feeling. It felt like I had walked only a few steps and at the same time it felt like an eternity, but in reality I was out walking and reminiscing for hours. I don't know what was causing me to do so but I couldn't stop walking. All I could feel was a new sense of strength and courage running through me. Maybe it was life gifting me with adulthood, or maybe it was my mother that had gifted me with her strength and courage, but from that day on I was no longer the same.

As the days passed, I started to notice a greater sense of peace and calm come into my life. My perspective had changed. I was no longer letting the little things in life upset me and I wasn't taking my time with family and friends for granted. I could see with new eyes what truly mattered. Growing up with our ugly dark family secret had always placed a heaviness on my heart. I felt like I could not afford to be completely honest about who I was. I always had to look out for and take care of my family, particularly my mother because I felt she was the most vulnerable. Unknowingly, this was how she bravely chose to live her life. But, inexplicably, now that the heaviness was gone, I found myself smiling more, laughing and making jokes, which was unusual for my character. Up until then I had always felt like I was an old man trapped in a little boy's body not being able to experience what it meant to really be a little boy. Although I played sports, raced bicycles and motorcycles because they were my passion and outlet for my pain, I never truly felt like myself. Not until now.

I guess what I was feeling was a sense of relief no longer having to be "the parent" to my family. I had always looked out for them, worrying about their safety and what the future might hold for us all, and I never allowed myself to be a kid. Now I would finally be able to be myself, feeling alive and youthful, making jokes and smiling and enjoying life more, and even willing to find love once again.

Picking Myself Up Again

A Forbidden Love

Long before the loss of my mother, I had fallen for the most beautiful girl I had ever laid eyes on. Her name was Andrea and, though many may have called it just puppy love, I still consider it my first real love. To this day, I still think about what may have been if Andrea were still in my life.

We were just fourteen, yes, just kids. But even as kids we can feel love just as intensely, maybe even more so because we can love at that age without any baggage. We met in Bogota on a summer vacation. She was there with her family; her father was an associate of my father's and had brought her along. For me, it would be love at first sight and, during the short time we spent together, it felt like we had known each other forever. Naïve as it was, we promised to stay in touch an ocean apart.

I would continue to write to her a few times a week. Every time I got off the school bus, I would hurry to check the mail with anticipation yearning to find a letter from her. But there would never be one. My expectations slowly faded away and I would finally start to realize she was never going to respond to any of my letters. I had never held on to so much hope believing that we could overcome the distance between us but, regrettably, with each empty mailbox check, my heart grew weaker and the distance became too great to bear. Soon the years would pass, and I would continue to carry this heavy heart still hoping that one day I would hear or see her once again.

That day would come years later when I got home from school and my parents told me that Andrea had called. She said she was in town and asked if she could stop by to say hello. So, there I was, finally going to see my beloved Andrea again. I was excited but I didn't know what to expect. I truly did want to see her again but it had been so long and by now I had buried all my feelings for her in the depths of my heart. Once she arrived and I laid eyes on her once again, all those feelings found their way back out and flooded my mind and my heart with hope and love all over again. But it was not the same Andrea I remembered. Time had changed what had been between us; the distance had grown too wide and, without any explanation given or needed, it was clear that she had moved on and seemed very happy. No words were spoken between us. They didn't seem to be needed. I could tell that whatever we had before was no longer a part of her heart, so I didn't push the subject out of respect for everyone involved. Besides, it wasn't the place or the time. This would be the last time I would ever see her again.

To my parents she was very nice and pleasant, and they thanked her for the visit. As she walked away, I felt myself falling back into that old, familiar place of loneliness that I knew so comfortably well. I can't blame her for what had just happened because it was something that needed to be done, like tearing a band aid right off. We both needed this so we could move on.

Time would pass and I would finally learn the truth. Apparently, my father had been out to her dad's ranch in Colombia and was told by the couple that took care of the house that Andrea had never received any of my letters: they had all been thrown away. Once I learned about this it angered me but also gave me a sense of peace in a way. I now understood her actions that day, and I can't blame her. She was just as hurt as I was and it wasn't either of our faults. Our broken love was yet another casualty of our father's business dealings and ongoing feud. I would later come to understand why we were kept apart and why it could never be.

Michelle

I would eventually come to accept this and move on. Now some seven years after my mother's passing and for the first time in my life, I would find myself willing to live my life with a new sense of courage and hope. After a few attempts at love, I would come to give my heart to Michelle.

Michelle would come into my life after the passing of my mother when I most needed her. She would be the one that I would once again give all my trust and love to, unconditionally and totally. I never thought it would ever be possible after losing my first true love but here I was opening my heart once again.

Michelle was also Colombian and I met her after being introduced to her by a neighbor who had invited me to a party. I had already healed from a previous break-up and had mentioned to my buddies after being teased about not having a girl in my life, that I would start dating when God would send me a girl that was Colombian, of black and Asian descent, kinda taunting God and my buddies so they would leave me alone but also because naively I thought even for God this would be impossible. Well, I didn't realize at the time how wrong I was about nothing being impossible for God. Two weeks later I would meet this stunning girl of half Colombian, half black and Asian mix that would instantly take my breath away. I had always been infatuated with Asian culture and had a preference for dark skinned Colombian girls so my heart skipped a beat while I was being introduced to her and realized that her last name was Japanese, even though she said she was Colombian. After getting to know her, I found out that her grandmother was Colombian black and her father Peruvian Japanese, and that's when it hit me... I sure learned to be careful not to taunt or doubt God's power and the power of words. Michelle and I would be together for the next five and a half years and she would stand by me in the good and bad times to come.

My Mentors

Starting from the moment I was hung upside down for my lunch money to the more pressing reason of protecting my family, it had always been very important to pursue my martial arts training. This thought had always consumed me growing up and it would get to the point that I would start to train with my first Wing Chun/Chinese Boxing Sifu (Chinese for "teacher"). It all started when I wanted to fight my best friend at the time.

My father had invited my best friend from high school to come along with us to Colombia for the summer. He did and we had a blast. It was a great summer break having a buddy with so much in common to share my country and culture with, and it made it better than ever before. But time quickly passed, and it came time to return to America and get back for the start of our 10th grade school season.

On the start of the first day of school my buddy, who I thought was a true friend, started spreading rumors about my family. The rumors got so bad that they reached me before lunch time and by my physical education class near the end of the day I was fuming with outrage. It would have been one thing if the rumors he was spreading were true being that my dad was indeed in the drug business, but to actually make up things about what he had witnessed that were not true enraged me, especially coming from someone I considered a true friend. My family and I had been backstabbed for simply opening and sharing our home and treating him with the utmost hospitality. During my physical education class, I could not contain myself and I guess my anger was starting to get the best of me. And that's when I would meet my first Wing Chun instructor Sifu Brad, a quiet unassuming senior. He said that he would train me to fight my friend if that's what I truly wanted.

So Sifu Brad started training me a few times a week. I quickly became very proficient, only to realize that after months of training, I no longer felt the desire to teach my old friend the lesson I thought he deserved. Somehow, I had found peace within myself and no longer needed to take revenge for what had been said. It was my first real lesson of how training in the martial arts was not about learning violence but about learning to conquer and control ourselves. I could now forgive my old friend and no longer had the need to confront him and, even though we would drift apart through our high school years, we would eventually become close friends once again.

Along the way, I tried many different martial arts as well as jobs and a few small businesses only to find failure and frustration. It always seemed I could never find complete success. But then I met one of the most important mentors in my life, Sifu Ken.

As my martial arts instructor, he would become my biggest mentor and motivator in life. Up until then, I had studied many different art forms and disciplines but never had someone to truly motivate me to stick it out the whole way. I had always felt like a ship drifting in the wind' but this would all change once I met Sifu Ken.

During my studies with Sifu, he would refer to God in all his lessons and would constantly talk about how important faith is for a warrior and his survival. He would tell us that the difference between a good warrior and a great warrior was his faith. A great warrior has no fear of death as he knows where he is going in the afterlife. This makes him fearless and unstoppable and willing to die for his convictions.

I would normally come over for a regular one-hour private lesson. But my martial arts lessons would slowly grow into full on theology lessons, with Sifu bringing out stacks of books comparing all the different religions and answering all my doubts and questions. And when I would start feeling a bit too cocky for my own good, I would ask Sifu to humble me. This was a common practice with us because we understood that a cocky or overconfident warrior is a compromised and weak one. He would remind us that there is always someone bigger, faster and better than us, and we needed to not take anyone for granted. So, in these rare requests, he would go about humbling us with his vast fighting experience and superior skills, which I was always grateful and humble to receive, although it could be very frustrating at times.

I understood the importance of receiving these lessons from Sifu and cherished them greatly. And let me say this: these sessions were not for the faint-hearted. We wore no protective gear most of the time and took each other to our physical and mental limits while forging and tempering our spirits beyond what we thought was even possible. It tested every ounce of fortitude, courage and strength in me; it tested my will, mind and spirit to the very core. If I survived without any broken bones and nothing more than a few loose teeth and some black and blue trophies, I would always be the better for it. Becoming wiser and, yes, more humble was the ultimate goal. In a sense it was a replica of life itself, humbling us along our way, chipping away at our arrogance and pride. This was how we trained, not for trophies or money and especially not for the inflating of our egos but quite the reverse: to become truly humbled warriors in life.

On one rare occasion, before we started our normal lesson, we got to talking about God. I guess I had a lot of questions, and although Sifu never jammed God or religion down our throats, he was never shy about his conviction and reverence for God. Up until this point, growing up as a Catholic, I didn't know or understand much about God other than what was taught to me by my grandmother Abigail and what I grew up listening to from the priest in Sunday mass. Having studied the martial arts for most of my life, I had also dabbled in Buddhism and many other religions, including the occult. I guess I had become what some would call a "new ager." But I still had many questions, and Sifu was always willing to answer them patiently.

So on this day we found ourselves spending four and a half hours of my one hour private lesson talking about God and faith. We never even warmed up or threw a punch, just sat on the floor having all my questions answered.

The following week I returned and, even though I hadn't even practiced any at home, I felt I had improved. I felt like I was a better all-round fighter and my session proved it. Somehow, I had gotten better. It was the strangest thing and I didn't understand it. But the only thing I could attribute it to would be my previous private lesson where we had spent all our time talking about theology. I had always known about the importance of philosophy in our training but had no understanding whatsoever of just how important theology and God was in our martial arts journey. This was what had always been missing and what I yearned for in my training and why I had always lost interest in the past. I wouldn't know just how much these lessons had actually touched my heart till much later when I most needed them, finding myself in a battle for my life.

After many sessions and private lessons with Sifu Ken, I would go on to finally complete my first black belt instructorship ranking in the Chinese Combat art of Chinese Boxing. I would continue my training with Sifu Ken till I moved back to college but even to this day he continues to be my teacher and greatest mentor. In fact, he would inspire me to go back to school and continue to always learn. He would always say, "The day you stop learning is the day you start dying."

And so, I continue to learn. I was so inspired by our martial arts lessons in the healing arts that I decided to work towards my massage therapy license and then my personal training certifications. In due course I would abandon my mobile auto detail business and start teaching martial arts, personal training and working as a Licensed Massage Therapist. Sifu's inspiration would eventually lead me to go back and complete my college degrees as well.

My Old Friends: the FBI

During this time the FBI would stop by from time to time and question me about my father's whereabouts and remind me that they would never stop looking for him even in Colombia. But I never said anything to them. I truly didn't know where my dad actually was. And I'm sure they understood that, even if I did, I wouldn't tell them anything. They never stopped watching me, and because they were well aware of my relentless training they would even accuse me of being my father's muscle or paid assassin. These exaggerations came out of pure desperation and as a result one of our attorneys politely resigned as our representative because they made him believe his life was in danger.

Looking back, it's humorous but at the time it angered me because I was nothing like they portrayed me and I would never intend to live the life my father did. That was a promise to myself and my mother after her passing, and I would keep my promise. They tried everything they could to get to my father by questioning family and friends and even co-workers as well as the usual surveillance tactics. But I refused to give in and stayed in town and held my head high even in the face of all the shame and ridicule we had all been dragged through. Only God truly knew who I was and that's the only thing I cared about. I didn't care what the rest of the town and so-called friends or anyone else thought of me. I wasn't going to let them torment me. It didn't matter because the only ones that every truly mattered to me that I had to protect were my mother and brother and they were no longer around. As for my father, he had made his own decisions and I wouldn't be able to protect him now.

Back in Colombia at my mother's first year anniversary of passing, my father actually showed up at the ceremony. I was shocked and nervous for him because I feared the authorities would most likely be following me everywhere I went as they did back in the States but I guess they still had no idea he had actually made it out of the U.S.

A Goodbye Hug

After my mother's ceremony, we saw each other outside and briefly talked and gave each other a goodbye hug. I believe we could both feel it was one of sorrow and forgiveness for one another, and we both knew that it may well be our last farewell. No words were said—they weren't needed. It was a long and strong hug, and I could feel his sorrow and pain and his seeming to ask for forgiveness. This was the only hug I could remember my father truly ever giving me. He was never a very affectionate father to me but suddenly, with this one hug, he fulfilled every single one I had ever yearned for. Likewise, this would also be my opportunity to make up for my absence and anger and resentment and ask forgiveness for all my sins against him. I had not been the best son and had failed to love him as he deserved. And, although he had not been the greatest of father figures I couldn't blame him for not knowing how to be a father when he himself had grown up without one.

This epiphany would come only a few years later as I pondered on all that my father had sacrificed for us, my mother, my brother and me. He managed to get us out of Colombia for our own safety because of the uncertainties after the civil war thinking only of our future during these times of unrest. To survive in a new land meant struggling to give us all the chance of a better life away from everything he ever had. He made the sacrifice of moving away from everything he ever knew and loved, away from his family, from his country, his people, his food and his music, to come to a new and strange land. But, as he saw it, this land of opportunity, a land to be safe and free from his family's ties would be worth it all. This appreciation would open my eyes and start the healing of the many scars that I had accumulated, not necessarily by my own doing but also because of my father's choices.

I felt this might be the only opportunity I had to thank him for everything he had ever done for me and to forgive him for not knowing how to be the father that I needed him to be. And with that final goodbye, I squeezed in every ounce of strength I had and every ounce of love that I had for him. I wanted to make sure he knew how much I always loved him and how much I would always love and miss him. And so I hugged him until I no longer could, possibly for the last time, knowing that I would have to let go. It was one of the hardest goodbyes for me. As a little boy, I had always wondered what it would be like to have what the other little boys in the park had. Now the very brief time we had together was passing us by and I would once again find myself being haunted by his absence. It's ironic that I had gotten used to not having him in my life, but now it could very well be permanent.

A New Beginning

The War on Drugs

By the early 90s, the U.S. was helping the Colombian authorities go after all the cartels of the time. So when my father returned to Colombia, eluding the FBI and the DEA that were actively looking for him (sometimes missing him by seconds), because he would always win the hearts of everyone wherever he went, this would make his capture very hard for the authorities. The locals would constantly alert him of anyone that seemed suspicious for asking about him. Because of the active "War on Drugs," it was proving difficult for him to get back into the business once again. Everyone was laying low and not doing any new business—at least not as easily or as openly as in the past. Everyone was on high alert and not wanting to be exposed, so business had slowed down; this also made it hard for anyone to come into their circle.

My father who was now past his prime for any kind of honest job would find himself resorting to his old ways. However, it would not be as easy as before and found himself once again on the streets struggling reminiscent of his seven-year-old self. With no options in sight, he would have to make do as best he could and reach back out to his family once again. But they could not be of much help either. These were tense and tough times. One day my cousin Sandra bumped into my father and was saddened by his condition and felt so bad that she gave him a few dollars for him to get by. This was such a contrast compared to the man who had always been so generous with everyone who ever needed help but now could not even help himself.

He once had been given an opportunity at the "American Dream" and had not known how to appreciate it. Now he would find himself back in the same place that he had fought so hard to get out of, virtually at the hands of the people that had always dragged him down. He knew this but had no other options. I could only hope this would have been the time for some soul searching, acknowledging his sins and repenting; but only God would know what truly laid ahead for him. Would a second chance turn his life around? And if so, at what cost and how far would he go to redeem himself and save his soul?

And then Tati came into his life.

A New Love

Tati, short for Tatiana, was a young vivacious and warm-hearted girl that would come to steal my father's heart. She was the youngest of five siblings and would always find herself having to entertain my father when one of her older sisters would avoid my father when he came by to visit. At first it was out of courtesy, then out of pity because she felt bad that her older sister would always stand him up. But soon she would find herself looking forward to his visits and so would her father and mother who became very fond of him. One day she realized that she had fallen for this much older, interesting, unassuming man and, with the blessing of her father and mother, they married.

Now you would assume that a young girl falling in love with an older man, with nothing to offer her but pain and misery was only using him to move out of her parents' home. But, as it turns out, we would all be wrong. They would end up living with her parents because my father had nothing to offer her at first; but this did not matter to Tati. By now, the whole family had accepted him—faults and all—and grown to love this man especially his loving Tati. They were all inseparable, especially my father and hers. Mutual respect and a strong bond developed between them. Her father was a retired military police officer and was aware of my father's past—all of it. Nevertheless, my father grew to trust all of them.

Standing by Her Man

Tati would quickly become fiercely protective of herself and my father. She even learned to drive defensively and was always on the alert, prepared for whatever may come their way by any means. She had grown to be a strong valiant woman notwithstanding the reproaches of her own brother and sisters, worried for her safety. But to her there was no other option: this was the man she had chosen to love and stand by, no matter what. And her love would prove itself beyond very soon.

Early one morning on Father's Day, while staying at an old ranch home, they were awakened by screams from a man outside yelling, "Dágoberto, we are here on behalf of your former associate to kill you!" My father quickly got up, grabbed Tati and the little boy that they had been baby-sitting and rushed them upstairs onto the roof. He then returned for his ammunition boxes in the room but not before a grenade flew through the open window onto the floor of their bedroom. Seeing this, he quickly snatched the ammo boxes and ran up the stairway to the roof top as fast as he could, narrowly escaping the blast of the grenade going off behind him.

He would hold them off from about midnight till sunrise. With about half a dozen men shooting at the house and up at them on top of the roof, he valiantly fought back the whole night. He would run to one side of the roof and shoot a couple of rounds, then run to the other side and do the same, repeating this all night till dawn to make it seem like there were more men with him. These assassins even tried getting up the stairways that led up to the roof, but my father fended them off by shooting down at them, hitting one of them in the leg.

Eventually, by daybreak he noticed he was down to only two bullets. He looked at Tati—cold, shaking and in shock of what was happening and not able to talk. But she nodded her head, in agreement to a pact with my father that they would use these final bullets on themselves to avoid being tortured in front of each other if overrun by these men. But just as the sun crested over the horizon the firing stopped, and all was quiet again.

Eventually, they made it back down into the house to find the bedroom partially destroyed by the grenade. The outside of the house had been riddled with bullet holes. They were thankful to be alive. The little boy was unharmed and safe now but Tati was still shaking uncontrollably and this would affect her health and ability to have the family they greatly desired.

Later that morning Tati's father would come over after hearing what had happened to try and console his daughter and offer any help. Afterwards he stopped by his old military police post and discovered that two military policemen had been rushed to the hospital after a shootout. One with a shot to the leg and had survived; the other did not make it and succumbed to his injuries.

It was now apparent that my father's former associate had paid off the local military police to have him assassinated. This was a common tactic used by the cartels, that is, paying off the military to do their dirty work, and this was not beyond his former associate, who had tried many times to get rid of my father. This was not his first attempt, and probably not the last. Despite this horrific event, Tati would still not leave my father's side.

Joyous News

After some time, things calmed down and they would receive the most wonderful news they could have ever wished for. Tati had finally gotten pregnant. They thought it would no longer be possible due to all the stress she had suffered. But God had other plans—marvelous plans—with a new addition to the family that would bring both my father and Tati the greatest joy.

Her name was Goretty and she would become the new love of their lives. She was a vivacious little girl that quickly won everyone's heart, especially my father's. There wasn't anything that he wouldn't do for her. He was the most attentive father, fulfilling her every little desire, and she was just as special to him. Their love for one another was evident to everybody that witnessed their bond.

They would become even closer as she got a little older, to the point where she couldn't sleep without my father not being home. One night she woke up bathed in sweat, screaming that they had killed her daddy. Her mother Tati called to tell my father that

Goretty was very upset because of a dream she'd had and to please come home. But at that very moment, my father was being summoned by a group of associates to a very important meeting that would alter the course of his life and everyone around him.

Living by the Sword

*Then said Jesus unto him, 'Put up again thy sword
into his place: for all they that take the sword shall
perish with the sword.'*

(MATTHEW 26:52)

Once my father saw himself struggling to provide
for his new family, he realized that he had no other
option but to return to his old trade. So he reached
out to one of his old associates that he had helped
get into the business. This man was now the head of
a large conglomerate of cartel associates in Bogota.
By then the war on drugs was winding down, and the
cartels were once again back to their usual business
of supplying the high demand for cocaine into the
U.S. Fully aware of all this evil, he would make the
same choice yet again.

CHAPTER 11

That Cursed Money

For the love of money is the root of all evil:
which while some coveted after, they have erred from
the faith, and pierced themselves through with many
sorrows (1 Timothy 6:10).

The generosity of my father and mother was well known. Even in the lowest of times, they always shared what little they had with anyone less fortunate, and in prosperous times they would go on to bless others even more. I remember watching my father one time as we pulled over on the side of the road on a road trip outside of Bogota, Colombia. We had just ordered something to eat and were met with a homeless bunch of young boys around seven years of age, the same age he was thrown out of the house by his mother. My father saw them hanging around hoping to get some leftovers after we left. He quickly asked all of them what they would like to eat and ordered six extra meals for them. As our food was served, he took his plate and gave it to them to share until their food arrived. He then had them sit down and eat with us. I don't recall him even eating; he was more concerned with making sure they were all fed and happy.

It was their way of giving back and easing the pain that they had experienced themselves. My parents' first little rented house after they got married was a tiny little shack that didn't even have a proper floor. Although the floor was an actual dirt floor, my aunt Deicy tells me that my mother would keep that floor swept so clean that you couldn't even tell it was a dirt floor. This was their early beginning. They knew the struggles of living in a very poor and corrupt country. Knowing their humble beginnings, I could see they were both doing this out of the kindness of their hearts.

Tati knew about my father's generosity too. According to her, one Christmas Eve they managed to scrape up some money to go to the store to buy some groceries so they could celebrate Christmas Eve together. When my father got back from the store, he told her that he had bumped into an old friend that was in need of the money more than they, so he gave it to his friend for his family. That was the nature of my father; if given the chance to put someone else first, he gladly always did. Maybe it was also a way to atone for his own sins.

I was also feeling the guilt about where this money was coming from and how it was not only destroying our lives but also the lives of the many in the clutches of addiction. I resented my father for it and everything that he would bless our family with. But mostly I hated the times that he would return from his escapades trying to buy our forgiveness with material gifts! I never wanted or asked for any of it and hated myself at times for thinking we were the cause of so much misery and destruction in others' lives.

So all the money or things we had never gave us the peace of mind and security that we yearned for. All I could see was the misery it had always brought my family and me. After my dad left us for the final time, and after his downfall and escape, what little we did have would all disappear. All that money and everything we had ever acquired by that damned life and money, was finally lost—every little bit of it in one form or other. Nothing ever seemed to last because of how it was gained, and I understood and willingly accepted this loss.

Letting Go

Four years after my mother had passed, and now at age twenty-six, I awoke one morning with a sense of nostalgia for my father. I remembered how much he had struggled to give my family and me every opportunity he never had growing up. He had the opportunity to make something out of himself and not follow in his family's footsteps. There's no doubt that if I had grown up in Colombia and under the same influence as my father, I too may have fallen into the same temptations in order to survive. Although I was never groomed by my father's family to be in the business it could have been a very short step to my own downfall. After all the "Godfather" (the mob boss) was in fact my true godfather who had presented me at my Catholic baptism as a baby. I realized how tough it must have been for my father and mother to venture out to North America and live through all that racism and racial profiling. To this day almost every single time I fly back into the U.S. I still experience profiling, and, yes, maybe rightfully so.

But I am not my father. I made a promise to God and my mother that I would not become the stereotypical Colombian to most Americans, especially after witnessing how much my father had sacrificed to give us a better life.

Eventually, I would have to come to terms with it all and I would forgive him. On that day I was able to let go completely of the resentment that I was still holding on to for having to confront every finger-pointing person in that little town that I had decided to continue to live in without shame. That day I would come to understand my father better. How could I hold any more resentment towards him for not knowing how to be the perfect father when he had never grown up with one? I could finally and completely forgive him for all his sins, flaws and mistakes. As I let go, I would also realize that it wasn't this country's fault or its people. All the pain and experiences I had lived through were the outcome of my choices. We all have a choice; to judge, to condemn or to forgive and love one another. These are the choices we all have and need to wisely make. For with what judgment ye judge, ye shall be judged; and with what measure ye mete, it shall be measured to you again (Mathew 7:2).

And suddenly, I was confronted with the reality that if I ever had to go back home to Colombia to live, I could not do it. I would feel out of place. You see, I had always felt like a person without a country; at times living in America, I felt out of place mainly because English was my second language until I finally figured out how to make the switch in my brain to think first in English, before I spoke. As I started to make this switch I felt less like an outsider.

In fact, as I got older, I started to notice that every time I visited Colombia, I would feel more and more uncomfortable and more like an outsider there. I had never gone to school in Colombia outside of preschool and had never mastered the language either. Because of this, I always felt on the outer edges, not quite belonging in either place, until the day I realized I was truly more American than Colombian. I knew more about the history of this country than I did the country of my birth. By now I spoke English better than my native language and I felt more American than I did Colombian. Of course, I will always love and appreciate my homeland, the people, and the food. But growing up in America I had become accustomed to the American way of life, the security, the opportunities, the music, the food and, for the most part, the graciously accepting melting pot of people that make this country so great.

I realized that I had slowly become Americanized and felt very blessed for it. I also realized that I was not about to throw away what my father had fought and struggled so hard to bless me with. I am grateful for this country and all it stands for and I only wish others could learn to see what they have. The saying, "We don't know what we have until it's gone" is a frightening way to realize what has been lost once it's too late. I am fortunate to have seen with my own eyes the stark differences between both of my countries and it is why I appreciate this country so much. It has given me the opportunities and security that my birthplace could not. It has taught me well and allowed me to live the American Dream that it holds out to all who dare to grasp it.

And so, I had finally let go of the resentment I felt for my father and of the resentment of being Colombian and having to be "the bad family." But, most importantly, I had finally let go of the resentment I had towards this country. I realized how grateful I truly am to this country for giving me the opportunities that my birth country could not, and I have my father to thank for this. But would my father get to see the fruit of his sacrifices?

That Dreaded Day

The day my father received the call from Tati about Goretty's dream would be the same day he would make his ultimate sacrifice.

At the time my father's only way to survive and provide for his new family was to go back to his old ways, and, as I had mentioned before, he had to seek work from a former associate. My father's job was now to pick up shipments of money coming back from the U.S. On one of these pick-ups he would be hijacked and two million U.S. dollars would go missing.

Many years later I would be able to arrange a meeting with the "Godfather" and I would learn from him how the events unfolded on that dreaded night. He told me that my father was able to make it back after being hijacked but without the money. He explained what had actually happened and that the cartel quickly sought out the men that had ambushed and hijacked the money truck. They were found and it turned out to be corrupt military police. They were tortured by the cartel to make them talk and they found out that they had been paid to hijack the truck by a man named the "Cowboy." The cartel quickly found him and questioned him. He talked and blamed it all on my father as the one who had planned it all. I believe they let him live in exchange for telling them who had the money, but after the meeting the "Cowboy" quickly disappeared, leaving the country. They then set up a meeting with my father, the same night that his wife Tati had called him and told him about Goretty being hysterical about a dream she had about her daddy.

The LORD is my helper, and I will not fear
what can man do unto me (Hebrews 13:6).

That night my father walked into the meeting ready to confront what may lie ahead for him. I can only assume that being the one solely responsible for the pick-up of the money, he knew exactly what he was facing, possibly not even coming out of that meeting alive. But, even so, he walked in and faced the man in charge. I was told that he was presented with a recording given to them by the Cowboy, which had my father sharing with the Cowboy what he did for work.

Death and life are in the power of the tongue:
And they that love it shall eat the fruit thereof
(Proverbs 18:21).

I can only imagine what my father must have been feeling in that very moment, hearing the recording and knowing he had been set up, betrayed and back-stabbed by someone he thought was a close friend. Now it was about to cost him everything he had fought to regain—his dignity, his new family and possibly his life. I will never know what was actually said at that meeting but I can only imagine that an ultimatum was given to him as it had been given to the Cowboy: produce the money or else.

The Cowboy had chosen to escape from Colombia with the money, leaving his family behind to atone for his sins. The cartel would send a message to him to return or they would take the life of his eighteen year old son whom they had kidnapped. But he refused to face his consequences and left his oldest to die at the hands of the cartel.

After making it out of the meeting alive, my father stopped by to say goodbye to a friend and handed him the only suit he owned, saying, "Here I leave this for you. I will no longer have any use for it." This would later be told to me by this very friend, whom I would later get a chance to meet and be gifted back my father's suit for me to keep. It would be a somber but grateful moment as I later pieced all the events together.

My father then drove the whole night to get back to his little girl who could not sleep due to the premonition about her daddy. His wife Tati would later tell me that he arrived that night in a very somber mood, not saying a single word throughout the whole weekend. This wasn't too much out of the ordinary for him as it was his nature but she said that this particular weekend he literally did not say anything. He only stared out at the window as he smoked cigarette after cigarette.

The sorrows of hell compassed me about; the snares
of death prevented me ... (2 Samuel 22:6).

I can only imagine what thoughts were running
through his head. What was he thinking...was he
thinking about his little girl? About his beloved and
faithful Tati that had never left his side even when
he had nothing to his name and struggled just to
feed them both? What was going to happen to her
and his little girl? Was he thinking about the rest of
us, the family he had left behind in America? Was he
regretting throwing it all away—a good life, a good
home, a good wife and children? Now he was losing
it all over again because he could not stay away from
that life. Was he looking for a way out, a solution?
What was he thinking? The pressure must have been
tremendous, knowing that he had very little time or
options left. Was he making his peace with God? Did
he ask for forgiveness and ask for protection for all
of his children?

I can only hope that he found some kind of peace in
his heart before his time would run out.

The Call

At the time I was working at a nearby resort and spa as a certified message therapist and personal trainer. It was a great job, which I enjoyed very much. On this particular day, I was called into the office and asked to call my family. I did, and was told by my aunt Deicy to come immediately to her house because of a family emergency.

On the way, all I could think was, "What now?" I was getting anxious wondering who else in the family had come down with cancer now. What was so important that I had to leave work and rush over to my aunt's house? What was this all about? Never did I expect that this would be the day I had always anticipated. Even so, it would be the hardest news that we would ever hear and something I could never have been ready for ...

The Final Drive

That fateful morning would come. Tati was not feeling well and asked my father if he could take Goretty to school. Without hesitation, he picked up his precious little girl and walked her out to the car, placing her in the rear right seat as he always did; then he got into the driver's seat and started their drive to her school.

What was going through his mind as he drove along those quiet streets early that morning? The drive over must have felt like it took forever with thoughts seemingly flashing between his past and the present, tasting the bitter uncertainty with every passing moment, feeling the dampness of the early morning dew hitting his face. Did the cold air remind him of his impending end? Was he ready for what he undoubtedly knew would eventually come? Was he hoping it wouldn't be done that day in front of his little girl?

My sister Goretty as an adult would later tell me how the events unfolded. On the drive over she noticed that two young men on a motorcycle had started to follow behind them closely, and then rode past them once they got into traffic. Then my father and she noticed that they turned around and started to come back towards them. My father must have already realized who they were and what they were up to. Once the young men on the motorcycle made a U-turn, were heading back towards them and were approaching the car, one of the young boys raised a gun up to my father's head and the next thing that my sister remembers was a white light enveloping her. She never saw or heard anything, just this warm peaceful embrace from this white light that had now totally overshadowed her. It felt as if time had stood still and, just as slowly as it enveloped her, it started to dissipate and reveal the horrors of what had just transpired.

The car lunged forward from the release of the clutch once my father's body went limp. Thankfully it crashed into the back of a bus in front of them, which prevented it from going off the side of the cliff. In that bus was a nurse that ran out and grabbed my baby sister and pulled her out of the car. She asked her if she knew where she lived and quickly flagged down a nearby taxi that had also witnessed the event. My sister gave them the address and the taxi driver immediately got her out of there and on her way back home to her mother.

As they pulled up to the house, Goretty got out of the car and cried out to her mother, "Mommy, Mommy! They killed my Daddy! They killed my Daddy!" Hearing her cries, Tati ran out to witness her four-year-old little girl covered in her daddy's blood and matter. She quickly grabbed her, consoling her and took her inside to calm her down and clean her up, while trying to stay strong and calm to keep from going into shock herself.

The following days would be the most difficult for my little sister and her mother as they struggled not only with the loss of my father but with possible threats from the cartel against them. Not knowing exactly why my father was assassinated and who was actually behind it, they were in fear of their own lives just as we were back in the States. This was the reason my aunt and uncle had taken my brother's and my passports away so that we couldn't travel back into Colombia for our father's funeral in case of further retaliation from the cartel.

The Man in Black

During the memorial, an unknown man in an all-black suit approached my father's open casket. He leaned in slightly for a brief second as if to verify it was Dágoberto, then turned around and left without looking at or talking to anyone else in the room. In that instant, everyone became fully aware who this man was and why he was there.

Tati could no longer bear the pressure and was becoming increasingly hysterical to the point of having to be put under the care of her doctor. She was a wreck and not able to continue to be at the wake. Her family would step in and finish taking care of everything for her including watching over my sister. In Tati's own words, "It was the hardest thing I'd ever gone through."

Confronting the Ineffable

As I arrived and walked into my aunt and uncle's home, I saw them as well as my cousin Sandra and my younger brother Eddie all gathered close by waiting for me to arrive. I could see they all had a somber shocked look on their faces but my brother and I had no clue as to what was about to be shared with us.

My aunt finally spoke. Although I can't remember the exact words she used, I recall her trying very hard to choose the perfect way to prepare us for the news. I could see the anguish in her face, the sadness in her eyes and could hear the heaviness in her voice as she told my brother and me that our father had been shot and killed. It was the moment I had always feared and the words I had always tried to prepare for. But now that I would finally hear them, they would pierce the very center of my soul. Every cell of my body imploded with the most intense agony—even more so than when my mother died in my arms—and the most searing pain tore through my heart. I could no longer contain it, and I released the most agonizing scream from within. After I cried out, I was totally and completely spent and devoid of any feeling, in a state of shock and disbelief. The day I had always feared was finally here.

No Greater Love

Greater love hath no man than this, that a man lay down his life for his friends (John 15:13).

My father had touched many lives along his journey here on earth and everyone that had ever met him would instantly fall in love with this humble brave man. This was not a man that would back out of a fight: this was a man of honor that would stand up to what he had to face in any given moment. I believe that before my father had left the meeting that Friday night in Bogota, he had already made his choice and accepted what lay ahead for him. I can't imagine my father risking the life of his little girl or even the rest of his children if he had truly masterminded the whole thing and really had the money. Knowing his character, I can only believe that he chose to surrender his life for all his children. That was his character: left with no choice, he gladly gave his life for ours.

And that's what my father did: his ultimate sacrifice for my siblings and me would be his final act of love. He was by no means a perfect sinless man, but who among us can say that we are? I saw how he struggled for his whole life in order to offer us a life not filled with pain and despair but one of promise and opportunity. He had always wanted the best for us and this is why his death should not be in vain.

Yet would I be different and resist the temptations that laid ahead for me?

Revenge is Mine

The revenger of blood himself shall slay
the murderer: when he meeteth him,
he shall slay him. (Numbers 35:19)

Hearing that my baby sister had witnessed our father's death and how close she was in the line of fire was more than I could bear. I became totally enraged and lost control. All I could feel was anger boiling up inside of me. I wanted complete and utter revenge for what they had done to my father and sister. How could they do this in front of an innocent little four-year-old girl? How could they take her daddy away in such a violent way right before her eyes? I had always suspected that my father's business dealings would eventually be his demise. Living by the sword would return to him as his ultimate fate but what I would have never imagined was my little sister having to witness his death in that horrific way. This I could not understand and it would almost drive me to my end.

The next few days were a blur to me but a plan was formulating. All I could think about was the pain and revenge I wanted to inflict on the assassins. I had made up my mind to go take care of the people that I thought had taken my father's life. I quickly broke things off with my girlfriend Michelle with no explanation given. I didn't want her to worry or know what I was about to do.

Now I could see how it was all converging. Everything in my life had led me to this very moment. I had always trained and prepared for what I thought I may need to do someday. That day had finally arrived. I was about to put all my preparation into action, calling in all my favors in order to be able to make it into Colombia undetected. This would be a one-way trip. I was prepared to not come back until I got my revenge. I had never been so determined. All I knew was that I had to succeed so that this would all end and no one else in my family would have to finish what I was about to start.

But it wasn't going to be easy. My conscious mind was tugging at my heart and I was still struggling with the plan I was about to embark on. I kept hearing this voice: "Vengeance is mine; I will repay." My need for revenge and my moral judgment were in the midst of the biggest fight for my soul. I felt like my heart was literally being pulled apart because I knew that what I was about to do would have broken my mother's heart. I had also read in the Bible, "God is jealous, and the Lord revengeth" (Nahum 1:2). At base, I knew revenge was not mine to take and that I would be letting my mother down. But, most importantly, I would be sinning against God.

But who was this God that I somehow had some kind of reverence for?

His Loving Mercy and Grace

Thanks to my dear grandmother Abigail, I knew who God was—well, at least I thought I did. Growing up Catholic, I was taught to have reverence mostly for statues of Mother Mary and Jesus on a cross and to call every priest "Father." At the same time, this was confusing to me because Jesus Himself says, *"And call no **man** your father upon the earth: for one is your Father, which is in heaven"* (Matthew 23:9). So, I had always been a Catholic rebel of sorts and even ventured into the new age scene.

Then about a week or two after the news of my father, my aunt Deicy invited one of her Christian friends to come over and talk to me about Jesus. Unbeknownst to me, she had recently accepted the Lord. Well, being raised to always defer to our elders, I simply smiled and nodded my head but everything this man was saying to me was going in one ear and out the other, not at all making sense. All I kept thinking was, "I know what I believe and this is very narrow minded," and so I dismissed the whole conversation.

But not long afterwards, I would find myself in a fight for my life.

It was a Friday night just before 9:30 p.m. I arrived home feeling a heavy burden on my shoulders and an agonizing pain in my heart and soul. It was as if my mind was in a full on battle with my heart and I was caught in the middle. The agony of this battle would get so intense that I could not bear the pain any longer. After reaching for one of my father's guns that I had inherited, I cried out to God, asking Him to take the heavy burden off my shoulders. I asked Him to take this pain away or else I would have to. I said, "God, if You are real, please take this pain away."

The truth was I was about to take matters into my own hands to stop the pain. And in that very moment, I suddenly felt this huge relief and the heavy burden of pain and vengeance instantly being lifted off my shoulders. I dropped to my knees. Suddenly, all my pain, anger and vengeance left me and, as I looked up, I saw a vision that was so undeniably real opening up above me. I saw Jesus on the cross looking down at me with the most loving but heart-broken eyes. Behind Him were dark clouds storming up as He hung from the cross.

HIS LOVING MERCY AND GRACE

In that moment, I knew that I had put Him there: all my sins, past, present and future had put Him on that cross. I understood exactly what He had done for me and why He was there, and I started to weep uncontrollably and cried out in gratitude, "Show me what the truth is and I will follow You! What is the truth? Is it Catholicism, Jehovah's Witnesses, Buddhism, Taoism ... what is the truth? Tell me, and I will serve You." He had taken the pain, the anguish and the vengeance away. I felt such a debt of gratitude. It was the most overpowering and undeniable sense of truth that had ever come over me, and I could not contain myself or my gratitude. I wanted to tell the whole world how real and how alive He is. I wanted to climb the highest mountain peaks and scream at the top of my lungs, "He is real; He is alive!"

In an instant, He took away all my pain and my need for vengeance and saved me from my own hands. I was eternally grateful and overjoyed. I had never felt love like this before. His instant forgiveness, mercy and grace for my wretched and sinful soul was beyond my understanding. Jesus loved me so much that He took my place on that cross, for my forgiveness and eternal salvation. This was my instant understanding of what Jesus had done for me, for all of us, and my immense gratitude overwhelmed me. I wanted everyone to know how real is His love, mercy and forgiving grace.

For God so loved the world, that he gave his only begotten Son, that whosoever believeth in him should not perish, but have everlasting life (John 3:16).

It Was All Planned

Jesus saith unto him, I am the way, the truth, and the life; no man cometh unto the Father, but by me (John 14:6).

The next morning while I was managing the local gym and training my clients, one of our employees that babysat the members' kids came in as usual. She always had that smiling but quiet demeanor. After her shift, Julie approached me and asked if I liked to dance and I replied, "Of course! I'm Latino. I'm not very good but I love it; it's in my blood."

She responded, "Great, let's go dancing tonight. I'll pick you up."

"Great, I'll see you tonight," I said. I didn't give much thought to the fact that it was the first time we'd ever had a conversation because I thought she was just a very private or shy person. But I was still feeling overwhelmed with my newfound inner happiness.

So that night Julie picked me up and we drove to a popular club in the downtown area. It happened to be Mardi Gras night at the club. However, not very long after being there, we kinda both looked at each other and Julie said to me, "You're not really feeling this place are you?"

I replied, "Not really."

"You want to go get a cup of coffee at the nearby diner?" she offered.

"Yes, let's go!"

On the drive over to the diner I could not avoid looking at her and I kept asking God, "God, why does she look like she's constantly smiling, even when she is not?" I was mesmerized by her and couldn't understand why. As we sat down and ordered our drinks, I couldn't keep myself from staring at her and thinking why she looks that way. Finally, I couldn't stop myself and asked, "Julie, why do you look like you're always smiling even when you're not?"

She replied, "That's called Joy."

Confused, I asked, "What do you mean?"

She answered, "Happiness is manmade and temporary but Joy is eternal and comes from God. You see, I used to be a very different person a few years back but God saved me when I gave my life to Him."

Then I said, "I gave my life to Him last night."

And she replied, "I know; that's why we are here tonight ... the Lord spoke to me last night just before 9:30 p.m. and told me to pray for you and to invite you out tonight."

I was speechless and still to this day I get goose bumps every time I think or speak about it. She asked me if I had prayed the Sinner's prayer and I said, "No, I don't know the prayer." And so we proceeded to hold hands right there at the table in this popular diner on a Saturday night with not a care who was watching, and I repeated the Sinner's prayer out loud.

As we finished, I said to Julie, "Julie, I just realized I had prayed this exact prayer last night not understanding what I was saying, but it was the exact words."

I couldn't believe what was happening. In my darkest moment, here I am getting ready to end my pain. Then I ask God to take my pain away and He did. I ask Him to tell me what the truth was, and He sends Julie into my life to guide me with the truth. I hadn't realized it but I had actually prayed the exact prayer by myself as if the Holy Spirit had guided me the night before.

> *Howbeit when he, the Spirit of truth, is come, he will guide you into all truth: for he shall not speak of himself; but whatsoever he shall hear, that shall he speak: and he will shew you things to come (John 16:13).*

The following Monday was my day off but they needed me back to help find a lost document. I unwillingly made it back to the gym and as I walked in, to my surprise, my dearest of childhood friends Eric was there to surprise me. I hadn't seen him in ten years and was so happy to see my buddy once again. It had all been a ploy to get me to come into the gym so my friend Eric could surprise me and it worked. Eric was my best friend growing up. We had met in elementary school and we bonded over motorcycles and BMX (bicycle motocross). The last time I had spent any time with him was soon after my mother had passed away and I was on tour racing BMX and we met at a few of the races. Unfortunately, I was not in the right frame of mind dealing with my mother's loss, but I figured it was a good way to get my mind off things. But I quickly found I was in no condition to be around other people, let alone racing. My buddy Eric, though was still very gracious and put up with my mood. I always admired his commitment to God and the change in him since he was saved. So you can imagine when I saw him, how excited I was to tell him the good news.

Therefore if any man be in Christ,
he is a new creature: old things are passed away;
behold, all things are become new
(2 Corinthians 5:17).

We decided to grab some lunch and on the way, I told him that I had given my life to the Lord that past Friday. He was very excited for me. I also shared that I was feeling something very strange. It was if I was dying or going to die soon; but I was okay with it and wasn't even afraid of how it would happen no matter the way—be it cancer or on my motorcycle. But what was really strange was that at the same time I was feeling something new that I couldn't explain bubbling inside of me. Eric instantly replied, "Do you know what you're feeling? You're experiencing the feeling of being born again. At the same time that your old self is dying, a new person in you is being born again. You are feeling being born again as a new person in Christ."

That was the first time I had heard what being "born again" meant and I was literally experiencing it firsthand. It made perfect sense: that's exactly what I was feeling. It was a most confusing, yet amazing and wonderful feeling. Eric asked me if I had been baptized yet and I told him not yet but that I had told my martial arts instructor the good news. He had asked his pastor if he could baptize me the following Sunday and was told he could and I was looking forward to it very much. I was excited about getting baptized because, as I had mentioned before, I wanted nothing else but to yell out loud at the top of the highest mountain, "God is real and very much alive." He was alive in me and this was going to be my way of celebrating it and sharing it publicly with others.

Jesus answered and said unto him, Verily, verily,
I say unto thee, Except a man be born again,
he cannot see the kingdom of God (John 3:3).

Now I believe that none of all this is pure coincidence. I had asked Father God for His guidance in discovering the truth and the very next day He placed Julie in my path. Then my martial arts instructor teaches me about the meaning and purpose of being baptized. And next my best friend comes into town unexpectedly and explains to me that what I was feeling was being born again as a new son of God and forgiven of all my sins by the blood of Christ Jesus. To me, there was no mistaking that God had answered my prayers once again and was leading me towards the truth since the night I surrendered my life completely to Him.

And he came into all the country about Jordan,
preaching the baptism of repentance
for the remission of sins ... (Luke 3:3).

The following days and weeks were all filled with lessons on becoming a new Christian. My brother Eddie and his wife and my girlfriend Michelle would get to witness my baptism as well as a client of mine with his lovely wife, who would gift me with my very own bible engraved with my name. What a touching gesture! It was a joyous day and I will never forget it. I felt I was walking on water. I was faith-filled with the love and grace of God and, although I still fail Him as I stumble and fall, I will always continue to seek His majesty and grace.

My salvation through God's saving grace saved me from destruction at my own hands. He took away all my pain and revenge and replaced it with eternal gratitude and peace. It's the greatest gift I could ever have received from God. And I now believe the white light that enveloped and kept my sister Goretty from being harmed and totally scarred from the events of that tragic day were God's hands protecting her. I am so grateful for God's loving grace on her. I know with all certainty God saved her and kept her from experiencing any deep-rooted emotional scars as an adult and why she is now such a happy and loving young woman.

CHAPTER 13

Who Is This Man?

Eight years later I would fly back to Colombia because my dear grandmother Abigail was seriously ill, and I wanted to be by her side. And while in Colombia, I reached out to and was granted a meeting with my godfather. As I had mentioned before he was gracious enough to see me and fill me in on what had transpired the days before my father's death. This was of great help to me in putting all the pieces together. This is when I would find out how wrong my assumptions had been and how vengeance was already God's.

Above all, I was excited about the opportunity to meet my little sister Tanya Goretty, now twelve years old, in person. Once my grandmother's health stabilized, I took the bus all the way out to Ibague, a charming quiet little city seven hours away, at the time, from Bogota.

The night I was about to leave, my dear cousin Nana stopped by to see me. In her usual spontaneous way, Nana decided to take off with me along with our adventurous cousin Diego. Great memories would be made during the next few days as we all met my sister, her grandparents and aunts. We arrived in Ibague late that night and found everyone still up waiting for us. We were greeted with open arms as if they already knew us. "What hospitality! What warm loving people! Such loving grandparents to care for my sister!" kept running through my head.

As they all introduced themselves, we were greeted with stories of my father and I couldn't help but be astonished at the level of affection they all had for him. I kept thinking, "Who are they talking about?" It's if they were all talking about a completely different man. I was puzzled and amazed at the same time, hearing all these wonderful stories of Dágoberto my father. I always knew how much affection people had for him but it was in the way they all shared their individual stories that showed me just how much he was revered and loved by everyone. I felt as if they were talking about an entirely different person that I never really knew. Maybe because we were "his boys" and he was trying to teach us how to become tough, strong men that I never got to experience this side of him. Or maybe he had turned a new leaf, or maybe someone had changed his heart for the better. There had been many women in his life but

I knew of only a few that could have brought about such a change, and his little Goretty was one. And now I would finally get to meet his little girl, my sister Goretty.

I didn't realize that I too would fall in love with this precious little girl. At first sight, I could see how much she looked like her mother but I could also see the resemblance of my younger brother in her. At first, she was quiet and shy but I could tell how warm and loving she really was. It would take the next few days for her to slowly warm up to me and start to trust me but on the last day of my visit she would finally open up to me. We made great memories running around her grandparent's little ranch home that looked like something out of a magical movie. On one of the days we went swimming at a nearby river but it had rained the whole night and the river water was all muddy. So in my infinite wisdom, I decided to act like it was spa day and we all started to plaster mud all over ourselves—not realizing what a bad idea this would later be to our digestive system, ha ha. But it was all worthwhile and made for some great pictures and lasting memories.

This little ranch home was the perfect place for her to grow up in. It was such a warm and loving environment with incredibly loving family members and pets all around. I could see God's hand had always been on her as it was evident by all the blessings surrounding her. I was so very grateful to see this and how loved she was by all. I could see that God always had a plan for her and that is why He had saved her from what could have been an even more tragic end on that horrific day.

And now I couldn't be prouder of her. She has grown into a lovely young woman full of life, joy and dreams that she is pursuing. I am also proud of her half-brother Sebastian who has been her and her mother's angel, protector and man of the house. Sebas is Tati's son that she had after she remarried after my father's passing. He has always been a great support and motivator to both Tati and Goretty. I have personally adopted him into my heart. I am so grateful to all of them, starting with Tati for her selfless love and new hope she gave my father throughout his last days especially in his darkest hours. And also my sister Goretty who gave him so much joy and love during their four short years together. I am eternally grateful to God for placing them both in my father's life. And my adopted brother Sebas or, as I like to refer to him—my little bro—who grew up hearing all the wonderful stories of my father whom he would never have the chance to meet, but only admire and learn to love as a father figure in his own life. Even with all my father's faults, he was still revered by them. I could never thank them enough. They have been a blessing in my life and it makes me so happy to know they share the same love for my father as my brother Eddie and I do.

Our father's life can be summarized as a life full of pain. Known for his noble humility he searched for the love and affection of those he loved and trusted only to suffer pain and disappointment, while those that truly loved him were always waiting for his return. I believe his pain was the reason so many who met him connected on such a deep level with him because, when he sang, he shared the same pain we all have hidden deep inside.

Our father is gone but the memories and the stories of him will live on in our hearts. His life will not be in vain. We his children owe it to him to become the very best that we can be in honor of all that he sacrificed for us.

Afterword

Eternally Grateful and Joy Filled

Make a joyful noise unto the Lord, all the earth:
make a loud noise, and rejoice, and sing praise
(PSALM 98:4).

I can never express just how grateful I am to the Lord for my salvation and to my family and friends, who never gave up praying for me. I am grateful to each and everyone in whom God moved to show me the way and guide me to the truth. I am also very thankful to have had a mother and father who loved me so much. Through all my bitter-sweet experiences, I am grateful for all they sacrificed for me. Without either of them, I would not be the man I am today. And I am also very grateful to this country and all the opportunities it has offered me.

Like my father, I am a product of Colombia. But I am also very much a product of this country that has shaped me and offered me so much, thus why I am here, to supplant my father's dream of a good, honest and productive life. But, most profoundly, I am a product of my Lord and Savior Jesus's ultimate sacrifice. God's mercy, grace and forgiveness is the only true reason I am here today. I am eternally grateful, for His love and a second chance to live a faith-filled life with my Lord and Savior.

He is real and He is alive if we choose to allow Him into our lives, and by faith receive cleansing and forgiveness of our sins. This is His promise to all who believe in His Son, our Lord and Savior Jesus Christ.

The LORD is nigh unto them that are of a broken heart; And saveth such as be of a contrite spirit (PSALM 34:18).

The sinner's prayer is personal, but...
Romans 10:9-10,13
says...

That if you confess with your mouth
to the Lord Jesus, and believe in your heart that God
has raised him from the dead, you will be saved.
[10] For with the heart man believes even justice;
and with the mouth confession is made for
salvation. [13] For everyone who invokes the name
of the Lord will be saved."

May God bless you all, in Jesus' name, amen!

Dad, at his happiest, on his favorite horse, El Niňo.

My stunning mom, posing for my dad in a car he restored.

In Loving Memory of:

Fred and Walter

References

Unless otherwise indicated, all scripture quotations are from the Holy Bible King James Version, which is in the public domain.

La violencia/Colombian Civil War;

www.latinamericanstudies.org/colombia/la-violencia. htm

www.britannica.com/place/Colombia/La-Violencia -dictatorship-and-democratic-restoration

www.globalsecurity.org/millitary/world/war/la-violencia .htm

Dágo meaning;

thinkbabynames.com/meaning/1/Dágo

explorebabynames.com/meaning-of-Dágo

kidadl.com/baby-names/meaning-of/Dágo

A Personal Request from the Author

Dear Reader,

If this book moved you, taught you something new, or simply kept you turning the pages, would you take a moment to leave a review on Amazon?

Your feedback helps other readers discover the book—and it means the world to me as an author.

Thank you for being part of this journey.

SILVERSMITH
PRESS

Serves new and emerging authors
to help them write, publish, and promote their books.
Are you ready to share your story?

Visit us!
www.silversmithpress.com

www.ingramcontent.com/pod-product-compliance
Lightning Source LLC
Chambersburg PA
CBHW042046090426
42733CB00036B/2643